Frances Ikedife.

CW01650640

Kandinsky

Copyright © Original Spanish edition 1995 Ediciones Polígrafa, S. A. - Balmes, 54 - 08007 Barcelona
First published in English in 1996 by Harry N. Abrams, Incorporated, New York

Copyright © 2003 Ediciones Polígrafa, S. A.
www.edicionespoligrafa.com
Reproductions copyright © Wassily Kandinsky, VEGAP, Barcelona, 2003
Text: José María Faerna
Translated from the Spanish by Alberto Curotto
I.S.B.N.: 84-343-0999-8
Dep. legal: B. 9.900 - 2003 (Printed in Spain)

Vasily Kandinsky

Ediciones Polígrafa

Kandinsky and Abstraction

Vasily Kandinsky is considered the founder of abstract painting, and any assessment of his importance in the history of modern art must give an account of how that central innovation came about. As often happens with "breakthrough" developments, however, the chronology of specific events is open to debate. For example, most scholars now believe that the small watercolor which is often considered the first abstract (or "non-

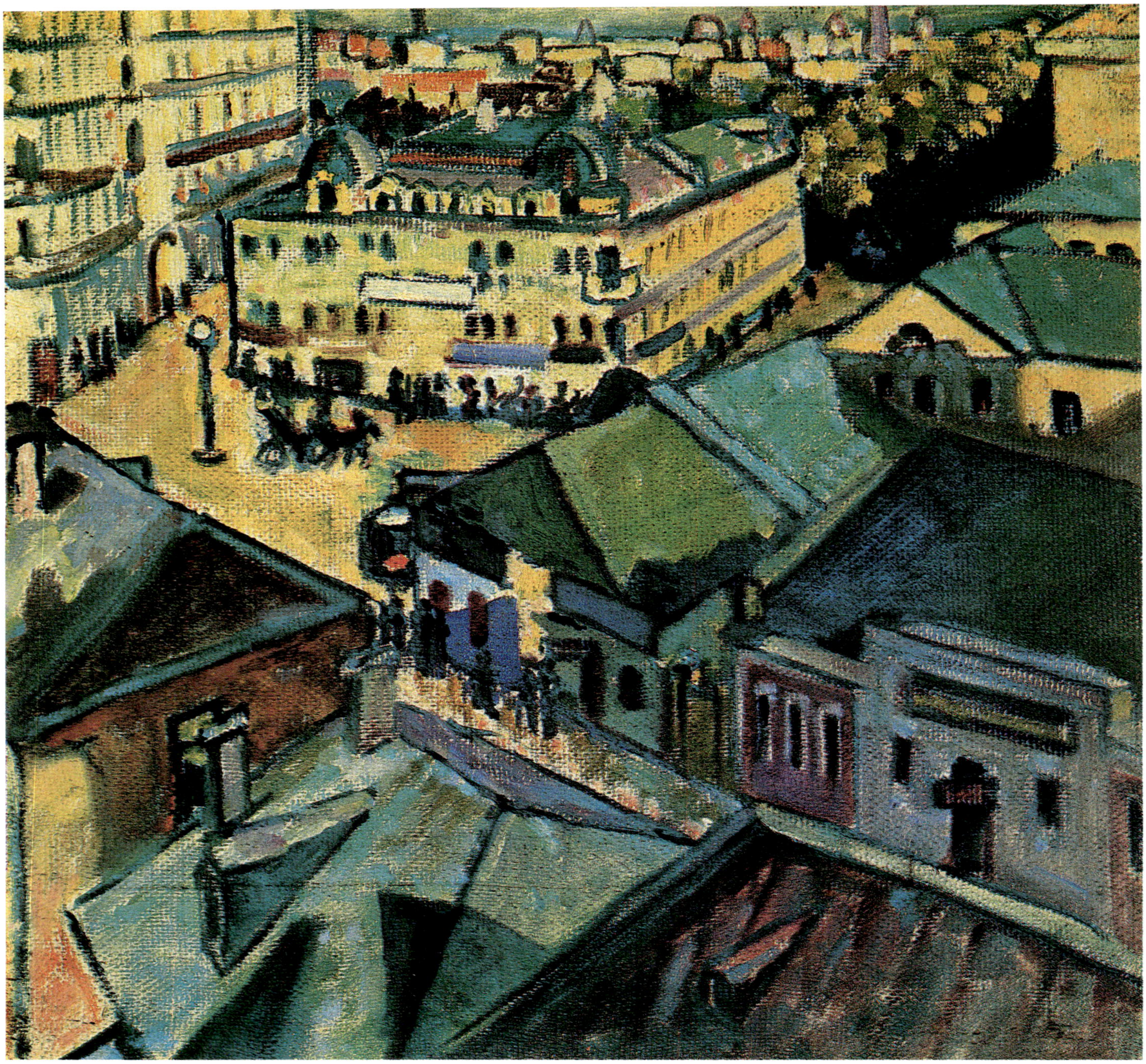

Moscow, Zubovsky Square III, *c. 1916.*
Oil on canvas, 13⅜ × 12½" (34 × 32 cm).
Museum Ludwig, Cologne

objective") composition—dated 1910 by Kandinsky—was actually made somewhat later than that. Moreover, there exist a number of isolated examples of nonrepresentational paintings by other artists from before World War I, some as early as 1910. But that is exactly what they are: isolated examples, not the heralds of a radically new aesthetic. For despite the complexities of chronology, it remains clear that Kandinsky was the first painter to "abstract" from the appearance of the objects of the world in a truly programmatic manner—the first to view the renunciation of the representational as a necessary step toward a purer kind of painting.

Varieties of Abstraction

Kandinsky was the principal innovator of abstraction, yet it is important to note that not all modern abstract art can be traced to him. His project was related to other avant-garde movements that emerged in the early decades of the century—Constructivism, Suprematism, Neoplasticism—which also practiced nonrepresentational painting, but often those groups pursued such experiments as part of a larger program, aimed at transforming modern society as well as the visual arts. Nor did the great current of abstraction that dominated modern art between 1945 and 1965, especially in the United States, issue directly from Kandinsky. Indeed, the primary inspiration for artists such as Jackson Pollock, Mark Rothko, Willem de Kooning, or, in Europe, Karel Appel, came not from the first abstract painters at all, but rather from such movements as Surrealism and Cubism, which had, in fact, refused to make the leap into the non-objective.

This, however, does not diminish Kandinsky's crucial role in the development of modern art. Although not all the varieties of abstract art descend directly from his work, his precedent made them possible. He made it legitimate to sever all ties to the "motif"—the depicted subject—and thereby freed the artist to concentrate on the paint itself, and on how its manipulation in lines, shapes, and forms affected the viewer. To liberate the elements of painting in this way has been one of the great aspirations of modern art, not only since Henri Matisse and Pablo Picasso, but since the time of the Impressionists. It was, in fact, the experience of seeing a work by Claude Monet that profoundly influenced the young Kandinsky and won him over to the cause of modern painting.

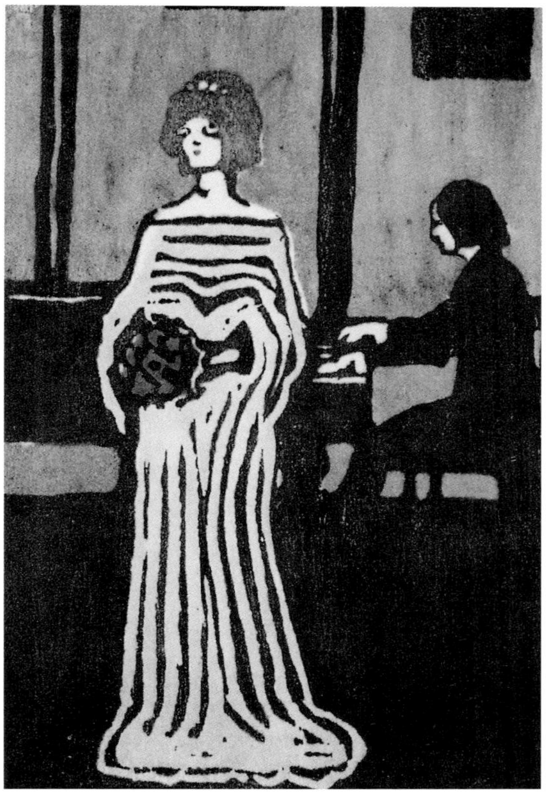

The Singer, *1903. During the first decade of the century, Kandinsky made his first woodcuts, executed in a Symbolist idiom.*

The Spiritual in Art

Though Kandinsky's mature work does not seek to imitate the appearance of the physical world, neither does it limit itself to mere decoration. Abstract art was not conceived as a way to produce pretty patterns for their own sake, but as a way to communicate more directly with the soul of the viewer. Kandinsky's art disregards the material world in order to attend more closely to the spiritual one. As with a musical composition, the arrangement of colors in one of his abstract paintings is guided solely by the principles of harmony and contrast, with the intention that this particular combination of elements will strike a resonant chord within the spectator. Kandinsky was in this regard following in the steps of the German and Northern European Romantic tradition, according to which the underlying subject matter of art, despite its many varied material forms, is always the unchanging world of the spirit.

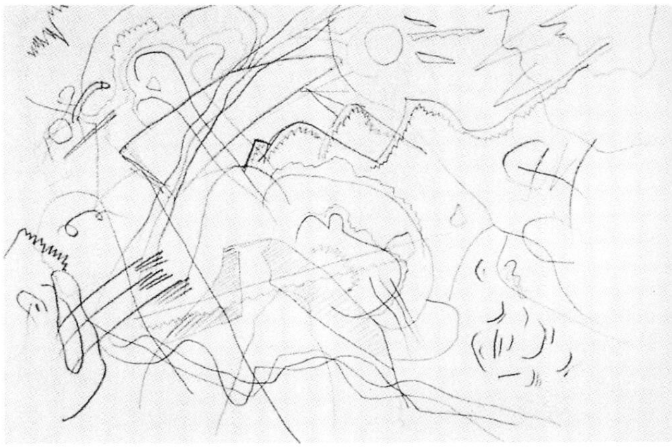

Study for Picture with White Edge, *1913. Kandinsky's studies are diagrams of the distribution of the color masses in the final work.*

Synesthesia

For Kandinsky, the comparison of painting with music was more than simply a metaphor. An awareness of his profound interest in music is crucial

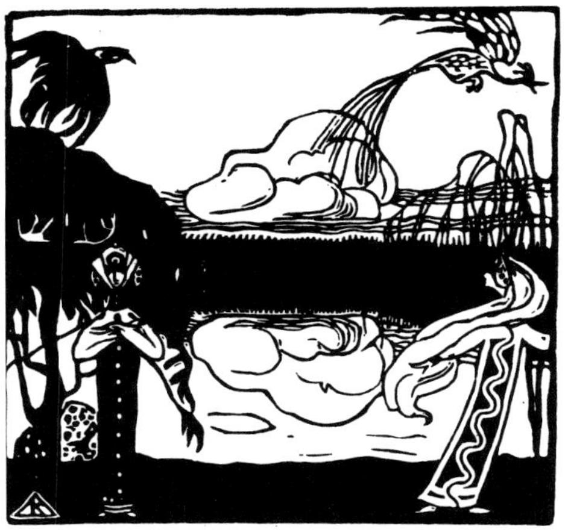

Two Birds, *1907. A clear example of the influence on Kandinsky of Jugendstil in Munich at this time.*

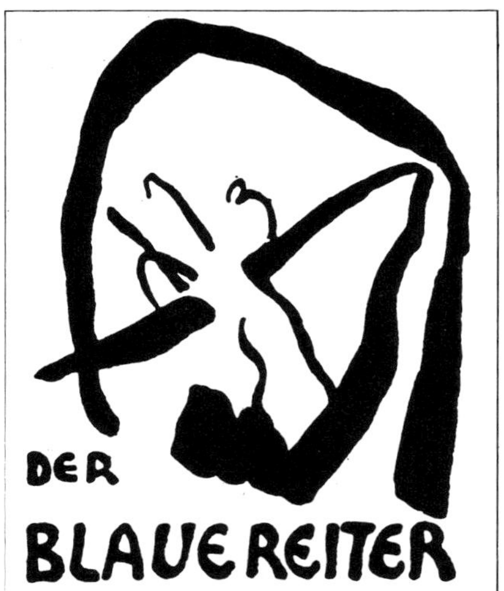

Kandinsky executed this drawing in India ink for the cover of the catalogue of the first Blue Rider exhibition, in 1911, a year before the publication of the famous almanac The Blue Rider.

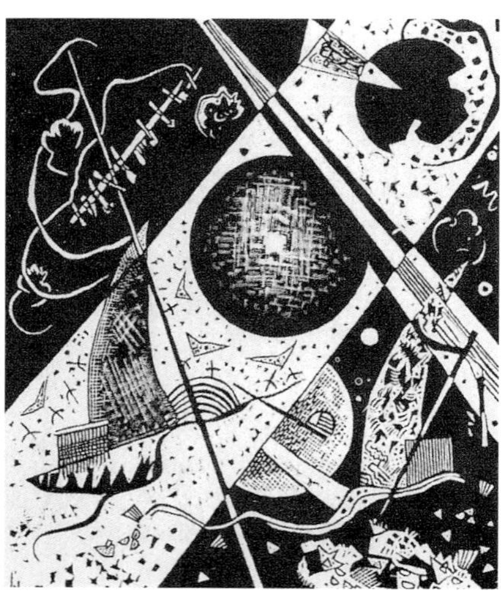

Little Worlds VI, *1922. Kandinsky re-created the world of his paintings in graphic works such as this.*

to any understanding of his work. The use of musical terms in the titles of his paintings, such as the groups called Improvisations or Compositions, is not gratuitous: instead, it conforms to the notion of "synesthesia," the idea that there are interconnections between the different bodily senses, such as hearing and vision, whereby colors are associated with specific sounds and musical harmonies on the one hand, and with particular emotional states on the other.

Kandinsky wrote about such phenomena in *On the Spiritual in Art* (1911), a brief treatise that defines the equivalencies between colors and concepts that are the basis of his painting. Spiritualistic ideas, derived from theosophy and occultism, also played an important role in reinforcing his ideas about sound and vision. But most of all, Kandinsky's understanding of the connection between painting and music derived from the Romantic operas of Richard Wagner. With his unusual interest in coordinating the effects of scenery and stage lighting with the performance of the score, Wagner conceived of his music dramas as a "total" aesthetic experience, one in which the visual and the auditory components would coalesce into a single, unified experience that would deeply affect the viewer's innermost being. As a result of Wagner's widespread influence, the notion of synesthesia became important for many artists, composers, and poets in the late nineteenth and early twentieth centuries.

The Aims of Art

Possibly because of his academic background, Kandinsky always had a penchant for theory, which led him to try to systematize his thinking about the ultimate goals of art through a number of discursive writings. Moreover, the awareness that he was establishing a new kind of painting increased his need to develop an intellectual rationale for his work. His years as a professor at the Bauhaus—the German school that in the 1920s and 1930s tried to apply the ideas of the avant- garde to architecture and industrial design—witnessed an even more thorough systemization of his theory of painting, notably in the volume *Point and Line to Plane* (1926), a sort of textbook for his classes. His more rigorous way of thinking at that time was not unrelated to the ideas of his Bauhaus colleague Josef Albers concerning the interactions of colors, and Kandinsky's work as an artist also became more disciplined in those years, pursuing a rigorously geometric style. Yet Kandinsky continued to seek the final significance of his paintings in the musical and emotional qualities that he ascribed to color. "Color," he said, "is the medium by which one can affect the soul directly. . . .The soul is a piano with many strings, and the artist is the hand that, by striking one particular key, causes the human soul to vibrate."

In this, Kandinsky strove to fulfill the old aspiration of the Romantic movement for a "total" art, one capable of transforming how we understand the world around us. Therefore, his aims were indeed related to the larger project shared by much of the twentieth-century avant-garde—to rejuvenate a broad range of human endeavor, beginning with the visual arts. Kandinsky's utopia, however, was neither social nor political, but spiritual. His ultimate goal was to facilitate what he called the "inner gaze," that is, a personal vision revealing the hidden soul of things.

Vasily Kandinsky/1866–1944

Kandinsky was born in Moscow of a well-to-do family, and although he spent most of his life in Germany and France, he always retained strong emotional ties to his homeland and its culture. During the first thirty years of his life, in Russia, painting remained only a kind of passionate diversion for this seemingly conventional young man, who was actually of a deeply Romantic disposition. After he completed his studies in law, his brilliant academic record earned him a professional position, but he gave it up in 1896 to move to Munich and devote himself entirely to painting.

The Early Years in Munich

The Bavarian capital, where the style known as Jugendstil was developing, was one of Europe's busiest artistic centers. Kandinsky studied painting at the Munich Academy and met Alexei von Jawlensky and Paul Klee, two of the artists with whom he would be closely associated. He also met the painter Gabriele Münter (see plate 14). The intense relationship between them, which lasted from 1902 until 1914, precipitated Kandinsky's separation from his first wife.

In Munich, Kandinsky organized a number of artists' associations designed to promote exhibitions. Phalanx, the first of these groups, was founded in 1901 and showed works by the Impressionists and the Symbolists, artists who had a visible influence on Kandinsky's early paintings. In the same years, Kandinsky began experimenting with woodcuts, a medium with a tradition in Germany going back to the Middle Ages.

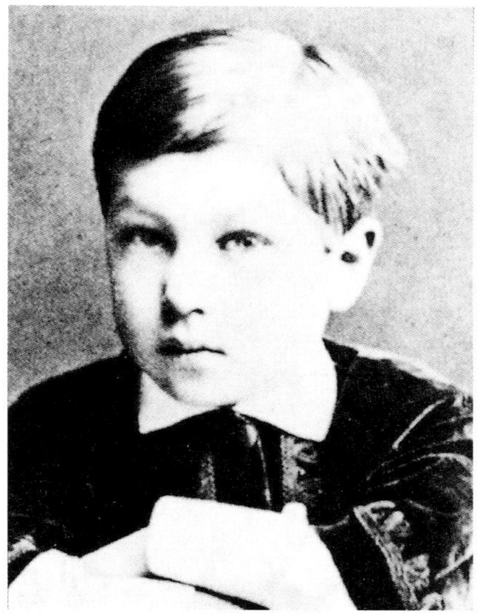

This photograph was taken around 1871, when Kandinsky's parents separated and his aunt took charge of his upbringing.

Developing a Personal Style

During 1906–8, Kandinsky traveled in Europe with Münter, exhibited at the Salon d'Automne and the Salon des Indépendants in Paris, and saw works by the Fauvists and the emerging Cubists. The irfluence of Fauve color can be seen in the works that he painted in 1908 and 1909 after settling in the German city of Murnau. At that time, with Alfred Kubin, Jawlensky, Münter, and others he founded the New Coalition of Munich Artists—known by its German acronym, NKVM. The ideas that would give rise to abstraction were beginning to form: in particular, Kandinsky pursued his interests in theosophy and occultism through the writings of Rudolf Steiner and Madame Blavatsky, which were extremely popular in European cultural circles at the time.

This period also marked the beginning of his friendship with the pioneer of atonal musical composition, Arnold Schoenberg. Schoenberg's development of a kind of music liberated from traditional harmony may have contributed to Kandinsky's development of a kind of painting freed from traditional representation. The composer may also have encouraged Kandinsky's thinking about synesthesia and the interconnections between music and painting.

During this time, the NKVM exhibitions presented works by some of the most important of the Parisian painters, including Picasso, André Derain, Georges Braque, and Maurice de Vlaminck. Kandinsky's work of the time, however, such as the study for *Composition II* (plate 22), still had not let go of the conventions of representational painting, although, in a manner somewhat related to Fauvism, its subjects were beginning to dissolve into

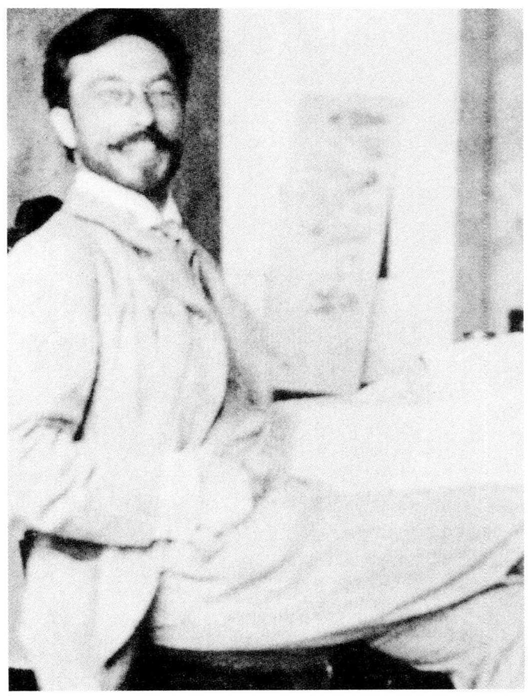

Kandinsky in Dresden, 1905. This was a productive period in the artist's life. In 1906, he would travel with Münter to Paris, where he remained until the next year.

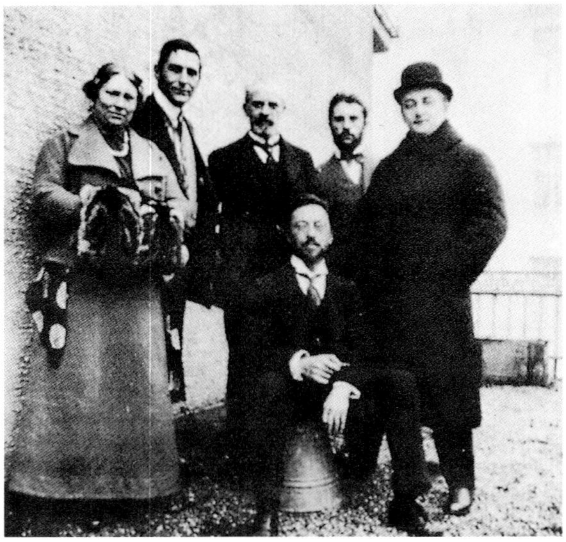

Maria and Franz Marc, Bernhard Koehler (père), Heinrich Campendonk, Thomas von Hartmann, and Kandinsky (seated), 1911.

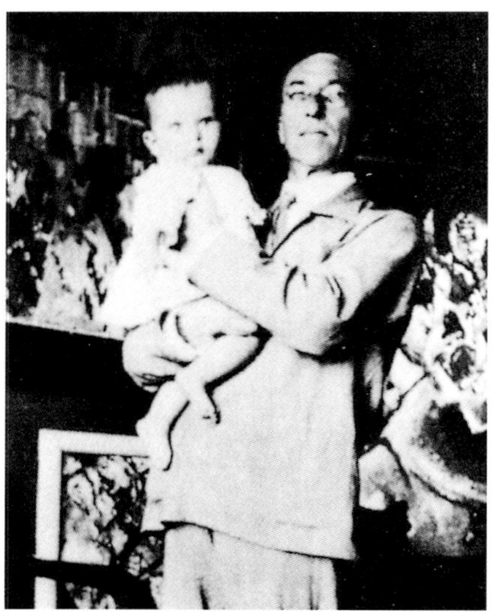

Above: Kandinsky with his son, Vsevdod, in Moscow, 1918. Below: The artist, photographed by Hannes Beckmann in Paris, 1935.

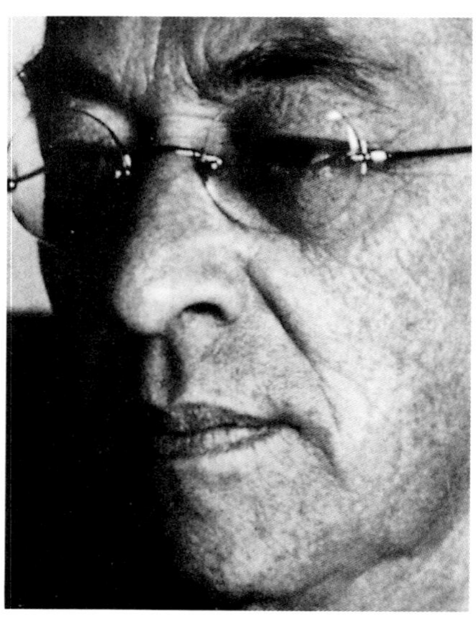

a vortex of colored shapes. Such works exemplify the ambiguous, transitional stage through which his art was passing at that point.

Exploring an Abstract World

Even this partial dismantling of representation was not welcomed by the NKVM. Kandinsky, however, continued to look toward greater abstraction, writing his treatise *On the Spiritual in Art*, published in 1911. In 1912, with Jawlensky and Münter, he left the NKVM and founded his last and best-known Munich group, the Blue Rider. In the process, Kandinsky met Franz Marc, with whom he collaborated both in the group's exhibitions and in the publication of an almanac, in which they expounded their theoretical principles and commented on the art that aroused their interest, from the work of such contemporaries as Picasso and Derain, to African art, to the Russian and German folk traditions. Among the other artists who exhibited with the Blue Rider were August Macke, Schoenberg, and the Parisian painter Robert Delaunay. Kandinsky was by this time working in a truly abstract mode.

At the outbreak of World War I in 1914, Kandinsky returned to Russia. There, the great upheaval surrounding the October Revolution of 1917 was also a time of artistic ferment, with the participation of some of the most advanced artistic movements of the twentieth century. Although his spirituality and his Romanticism were at odds with the prevailing materialism of the government and most of the leading Russian artists, Kandinsky held a number of important artistic and cultural offices in the administration of the new Soviet state. His efforts led to the founding of several museums throughout Russia and to the development of new educational programs. In 1917, Kandinsky married Nina Adreevsky, his second wife. Four years later, the two left for Berlin, and Kandinsky never again returned to Russia.

From Walter Gropius came the offer of a position at the Bauhaus, where Kandinsky led both the Decorative Painting Workshop and the introductory course from 1922 to 1933. At the Bauhaus, he found his old friend Klee, and with him Jawlensky and Lyonel Feininger. During those years, Kandinsky's work became more rigorous in composition. His devotion to color was supplemented by a new appreciation for geometry and by a more controlled interaction of forms, as his painting responded to the various stylistic currents at the Bauhaus.

Later Years

With the closing of the Bauhaus by the Nazis in 1933, Kandinsky was forced to leave Germany—his paintings would be among those included in the exhibition of condemned works called "Degenerate Art" in 1937—and he settled in Neuilly, near Paris. There he hoped to find a climate favorable to his work, but the French artistic scene was not at that time especially well disposed toward abstraction. André Breton unsuccessfully tried to win him over to the Surrealist cause and, although Kandinsky became a French citizen, the last phase of his career unfolded quietly, amid a general lack of critical understanding of his work. In his last paintings, Kandinsky drifted away from Bauhaus geometry and used more organic and biomorphic shapes. He died in 1944, too soon to witness the triumph of abstract art in the postwar era.

Plates

Formative Influences

Two events that shaped Kandinsky's artistic vocation took place in 1895: he attended a performance of Richard Wagner's opera *Lohengrin*, and he saw one of Claude Monet's Haystack paintings at an exhibition of Impressionist art in Moscow. Kandinsky's response to Wagner at this early date already points to the link between painting and music that would inform his work as an artist. And his response to Monet indicates something of his future course toward nonrepresentational painting, for it was precisely the dematerializing of the motif in Monet's painting, the way that objects were beginning to dissolve into color and light, that impressed Kandinsky, who was captivated by the work. "Unknowingly," he wrote many years later, "the inevitability of the object as a pictorial element was being discredited." Not surprisingly, then, his first painted works reveal the influence of Impressionist color, as later on he would be affected by the color experiments of the Fauves. In Paris in 1906–7, Kandinsky was able to expand his knowledge of many of the French artists, including those who had participated in the Phalanx exhibitions from 1901 to 1904—Monet, Paul Signac, Félix Vallotton, Henri de Toulouse-Lautrec—and those who would participate in the exhibitions of the NKVM: Picasso, Braque, Vlaminck, André Derain, Kees van Dongen, Henri Le Fauconnier, and Georges Rouault.

1 The Old City II, *1902. The mellow evening light gives a poetic aura to this view of Rothenburg, but the sharp, clear-cut volumes recall Paul Cézanne's paintings. Kandinsky's minute brushstrokes, heavy with pigment, make tiny tesserae of color. They suggest the perfectionist preciosity typical of many painters of that period, from Lovis Corinth to Gustav Klimt.*

2 Kochel: Waterfall I, *1900. The notion that a landscape betrays "the state of the soul" dates from Romanticism. Kandinsky may have been influenced by nineteenth-century Russian painting or by the landscapists of the Barbizon school. But more than these, the immediacy of this canvas, with its generous brushstrokes, reveals the influence of the late Impressionist manner that had left its mark on the painter at a Moscow exhibition in 1895.*

1

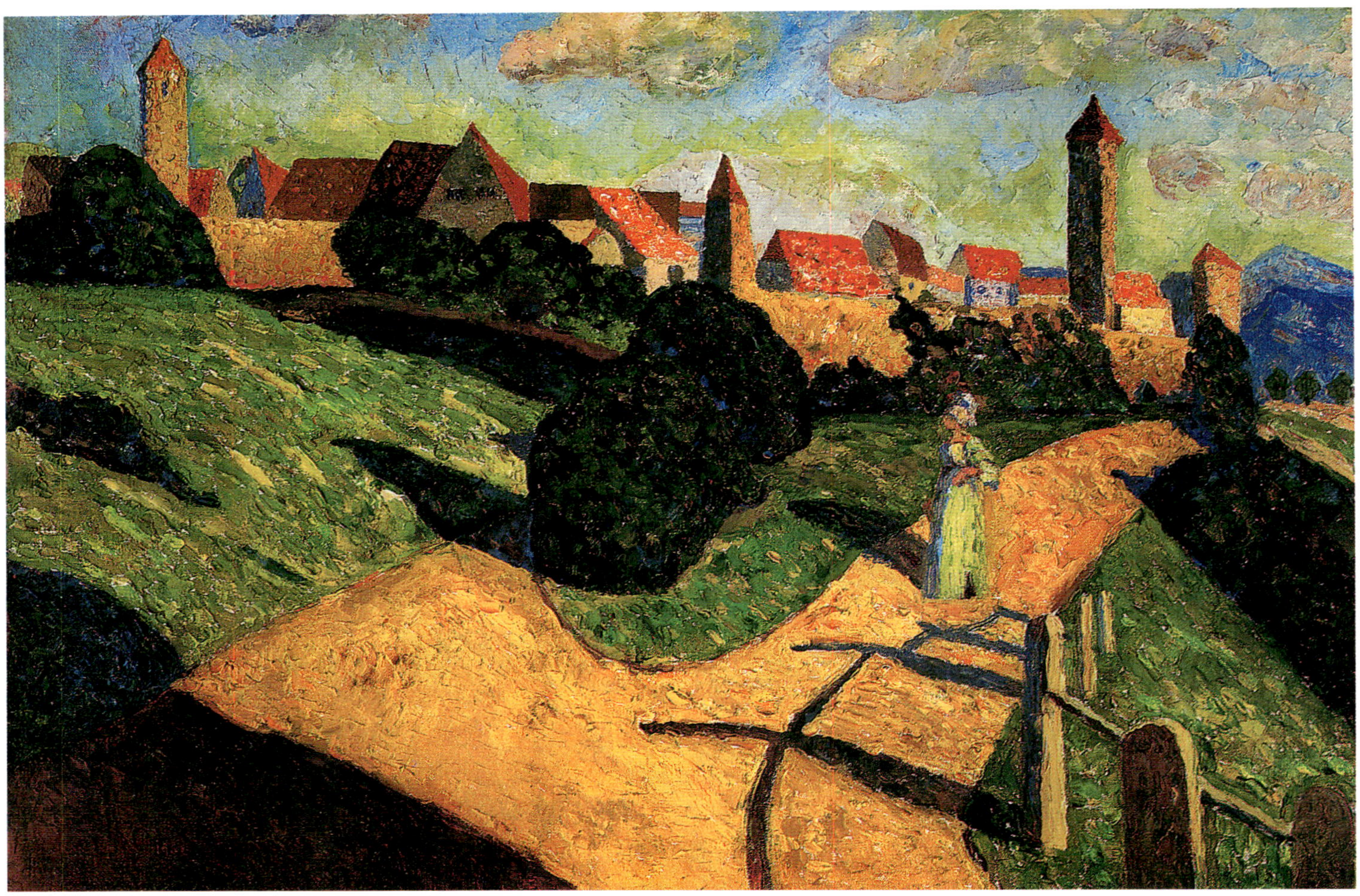

2

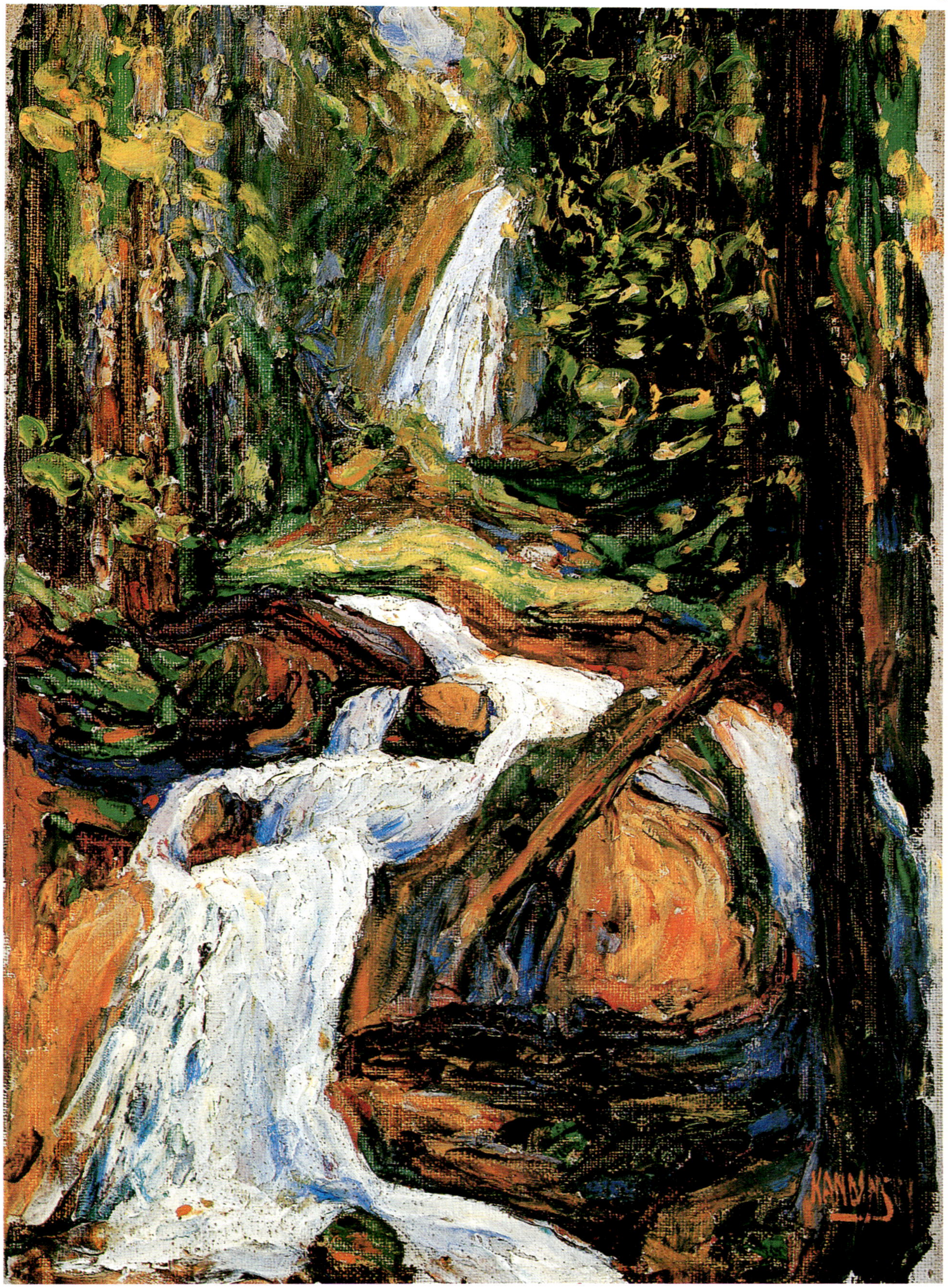

3

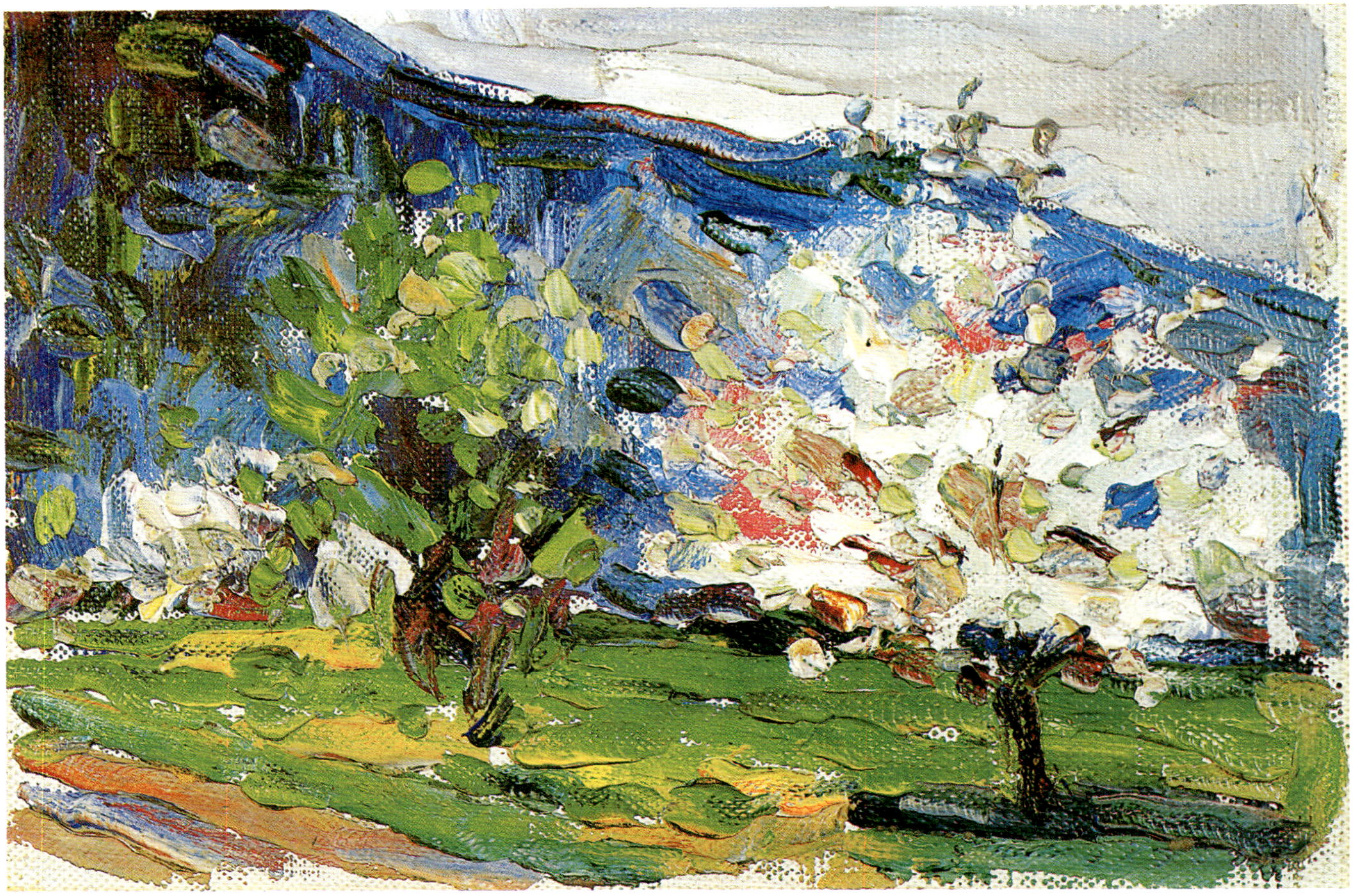

4

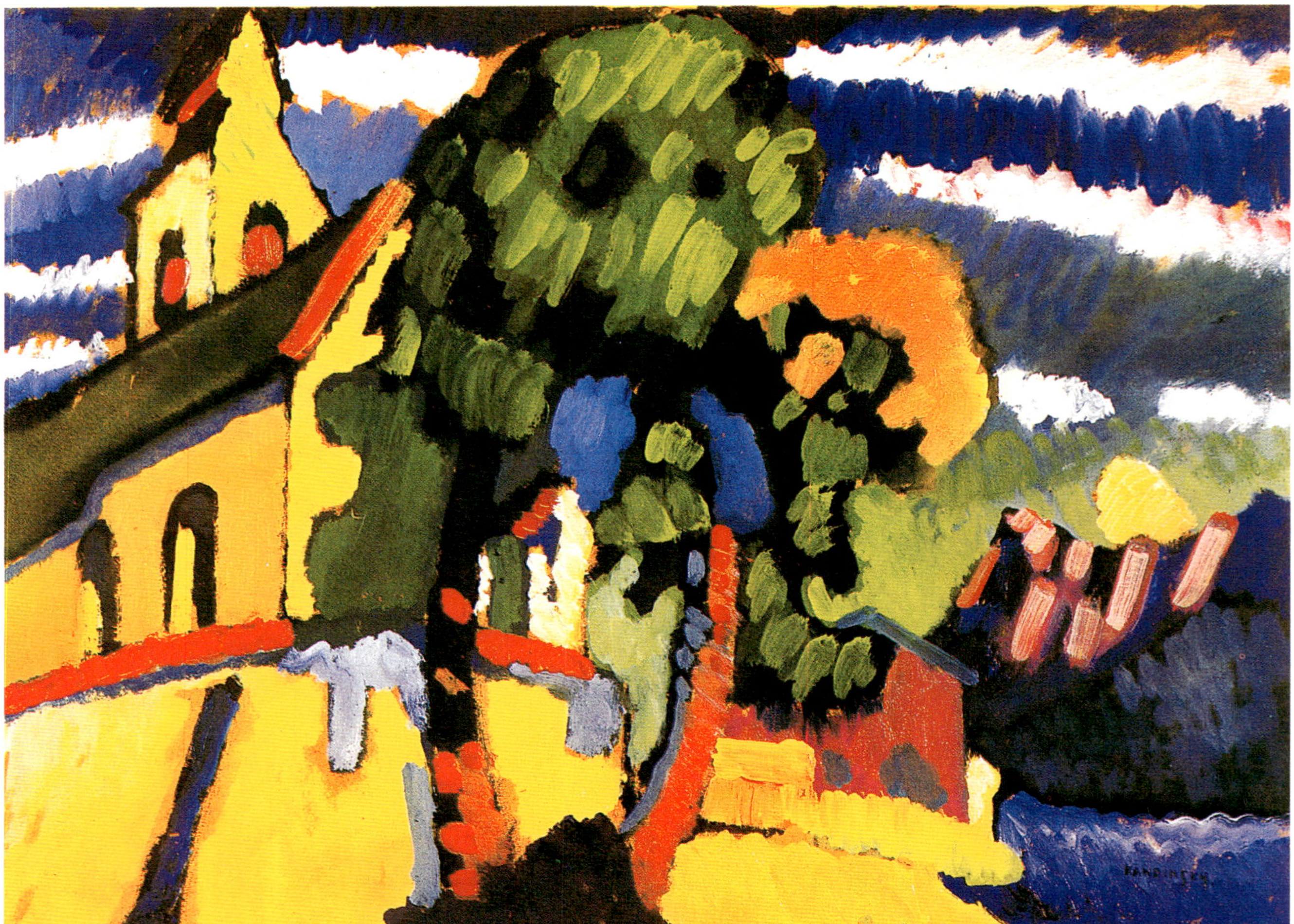

5

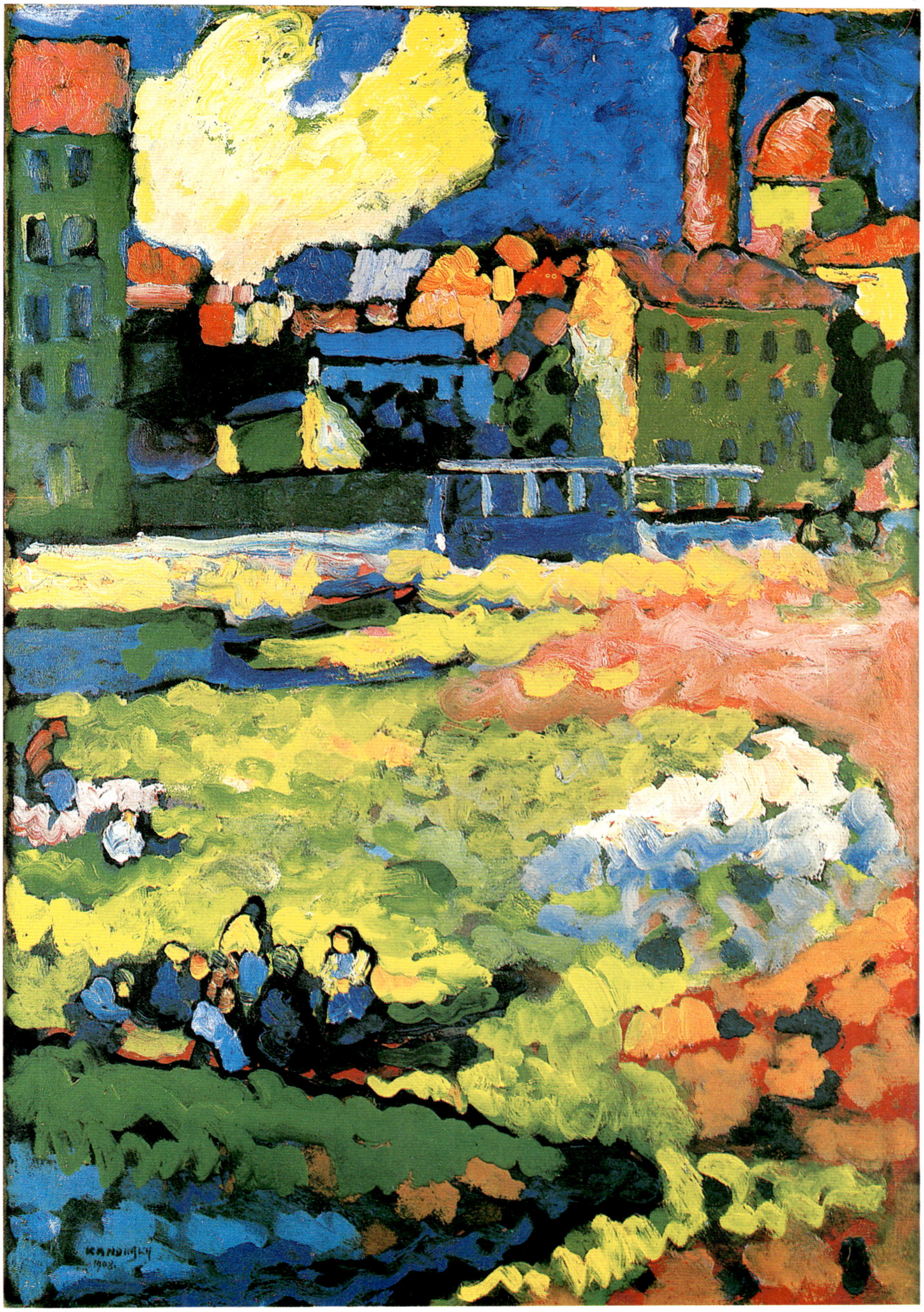

3 Trees in Bloom at Lana I, *1908. The intensity of the light green, made still brighter by touches of yellow, is a celebration of springtime, exemplified by the blooming trees. The projection of the artist's feelings onto the painted motif, going beyond mere visual description, is one of the most conspicuous differences between French and Northern European painting at the beginning of the twentieth century.*

4 Riegsee: The Town Church, *1908. The arbitrariness of Fauve color is one of the most important innovations that Kandinsky incorporated into his own painterly style upon his return to Germany from France in 1908. By emancipating color from the restraints of fidelity to nature, he took the first step toward pictorial autonomy—toward painting as a chromatic symphony.*

5 Munich: Schwabing with the Church of St. Ursula, *1908. Another striking example of the effect on Kandinsky of his encounter with Fauvism.*

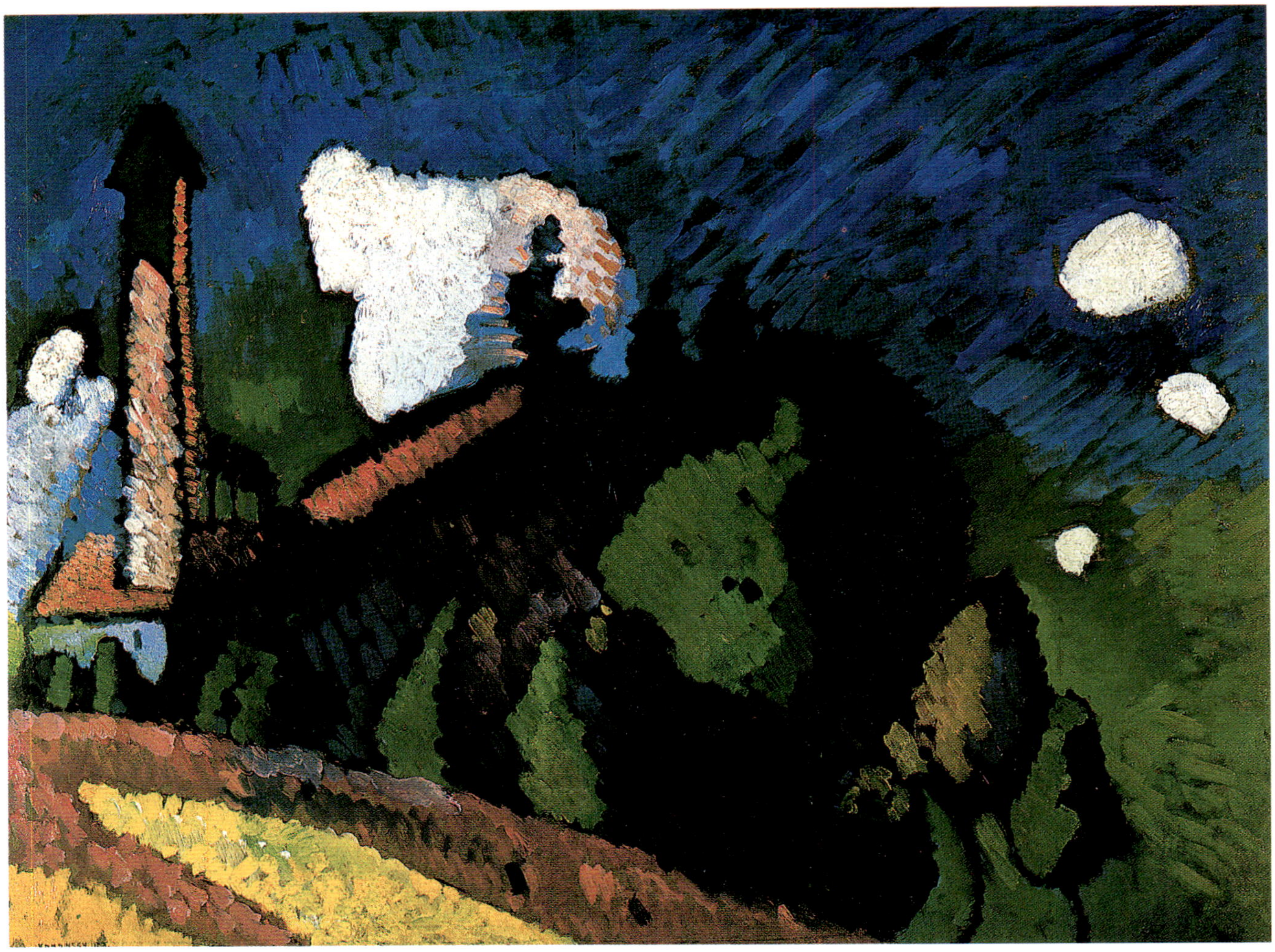

6

7

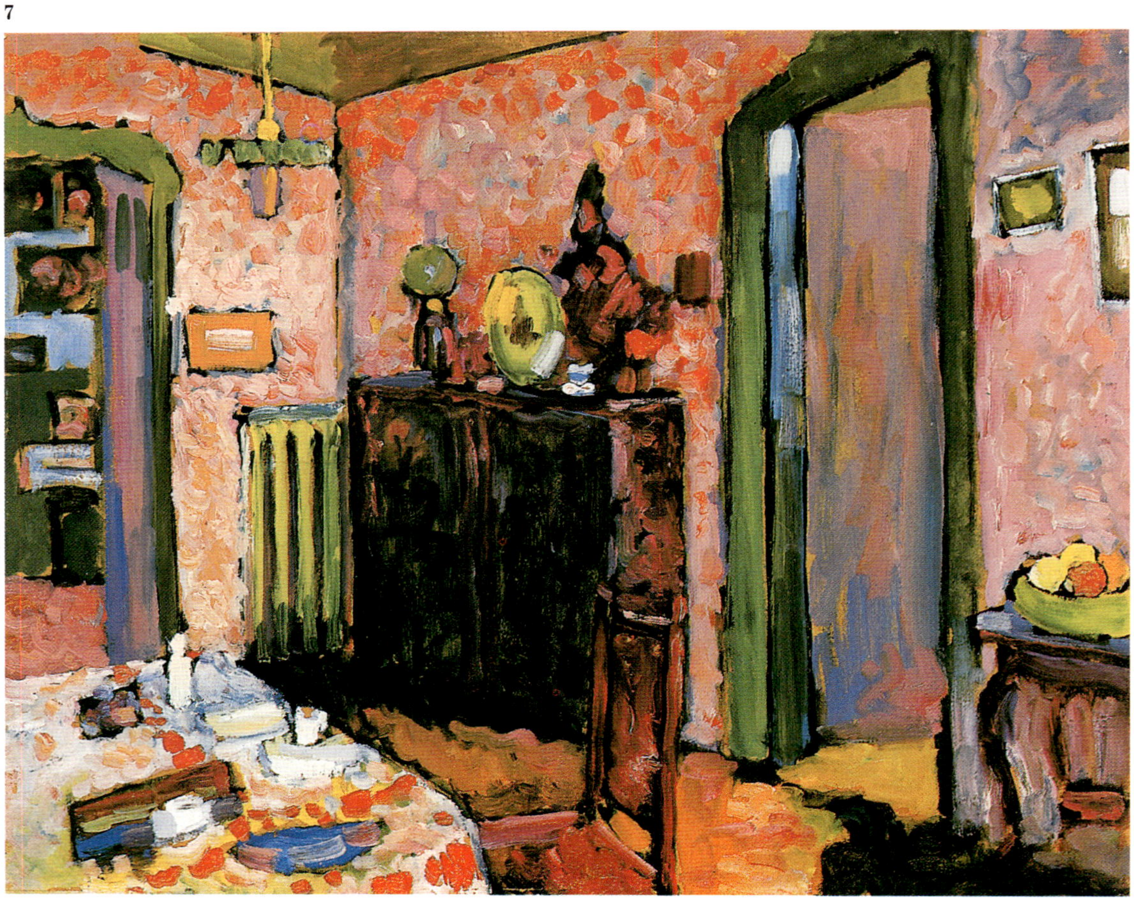

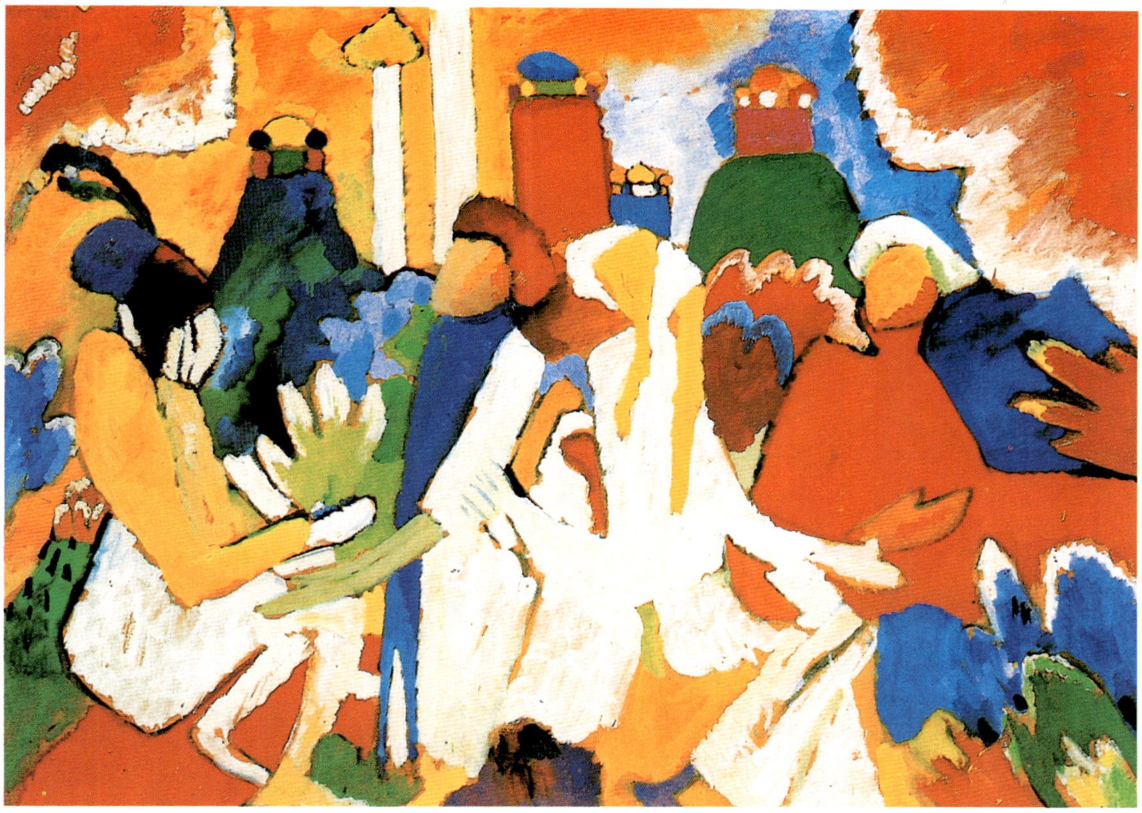

8

9

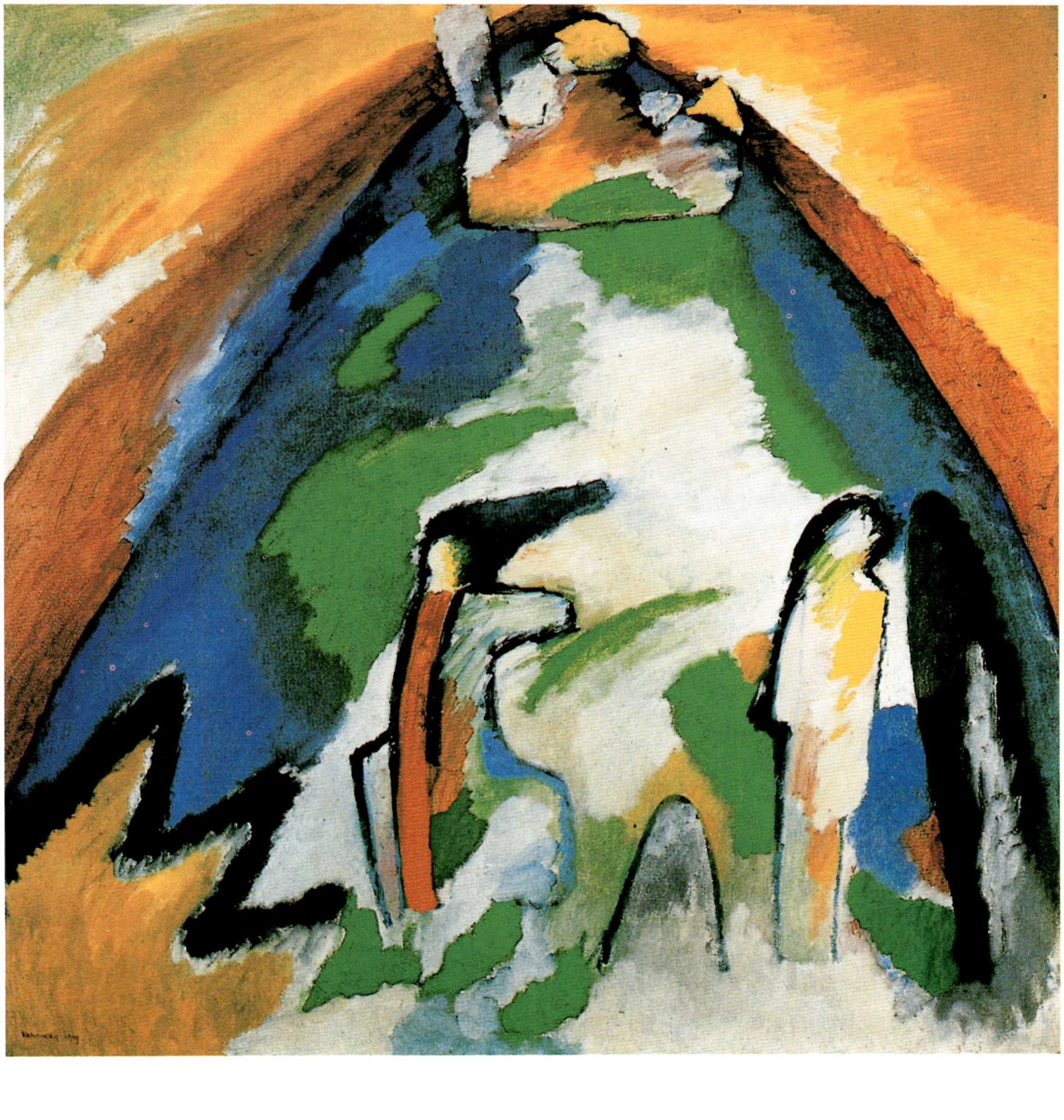

6 Landscape with a Tower, *1908. In this mysterious nocturnal setting, the pervasive red-yellow color chord of the brick tower, the roofs, and the field in the lower left corner takes on a somewhat spectral character.*

7 Interior (My Dining Room), *1909. The influence of Félix Vallotton, whose works were shown at the tenth Phalanx exhibition in 1910, as well as that of the French Nabi artists, can be seen in this meticulously painted, decorative interior.*

8 Oriental, *1909. Here, the coloristic exuberance of the Fauvists is beginning to overpower the motif, breaking free from it. The drawn shapes can barely contain the brashly vibrant reds and yellows.*

9 Mountain, *1909. The narrative element is downplayed in favor of a pure harmony of colors. Yellow, red, blue, and green—the basis of Kandinsky's chromatic vocabulary—here create a feeling of ascent, as he arranges the color areas with the brighter, lighter hues toward the top of the painting.*

Developments in Munich

In 1896, at the time of Kandinsky's arrival in Munich, the Bavarian capital was one of Europe's most important modernist centers. In 1892, a group of artists had broken away from the official academy and founded the Secession movement, which included some of the foremost painters of that time, such as Lovis Corinth and Franz von Stuck. The same year saw the first publication of the review *Jugend*, from which the German modernist style called Jugendstil took its name, and whose orbit attracted such figures as Hermann Obrist and August Endell. Their influence is evident in several of Kandinsky's works, such as his poster for the Phalanx exhibitions, but his strongest link to the Munich art world was his devotion to Romantic idealism, which had already emerged while he was in Russia. Kandinsky assimilated the melancholic tone of Symbolism, one of the prevailing currents of the Secession, and its taste for landscape. The inner correspondence of color with the emotions is part of this Romantic heritage, which Kandinsky combined with the influence of Fauvism.

10 Obermarkt with Mountains, *1908. This is one of the earliest works painted in the small Bavarian village where Kandinsky sojourned with Gabriele Münter. The pale yet luminous color confers an air of melancholy on the scene, which is treated with the sharp contrast of light and shade typical of woodcuts. The picture's style may also owe something to Ferdinand Hodler.*

10

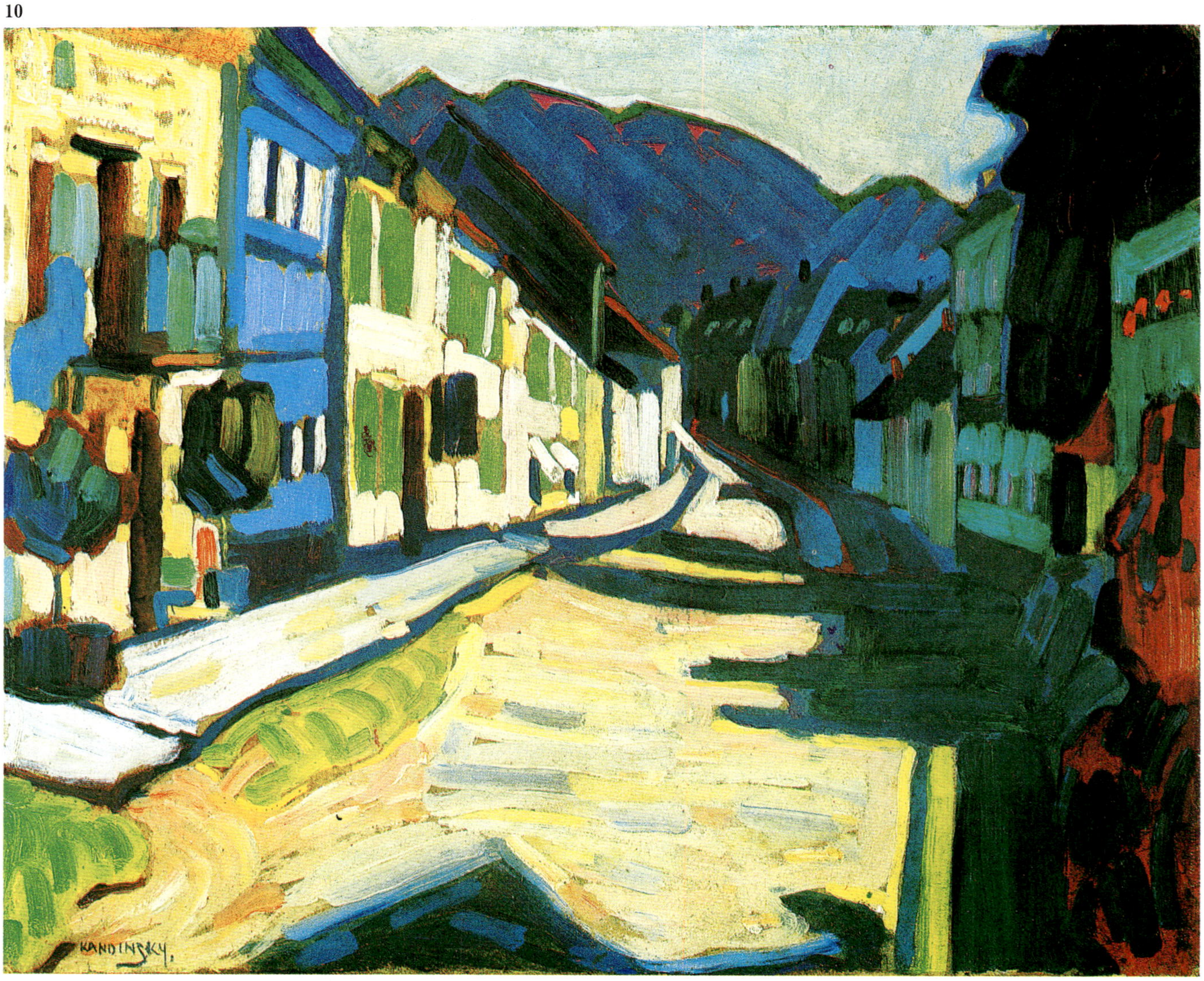

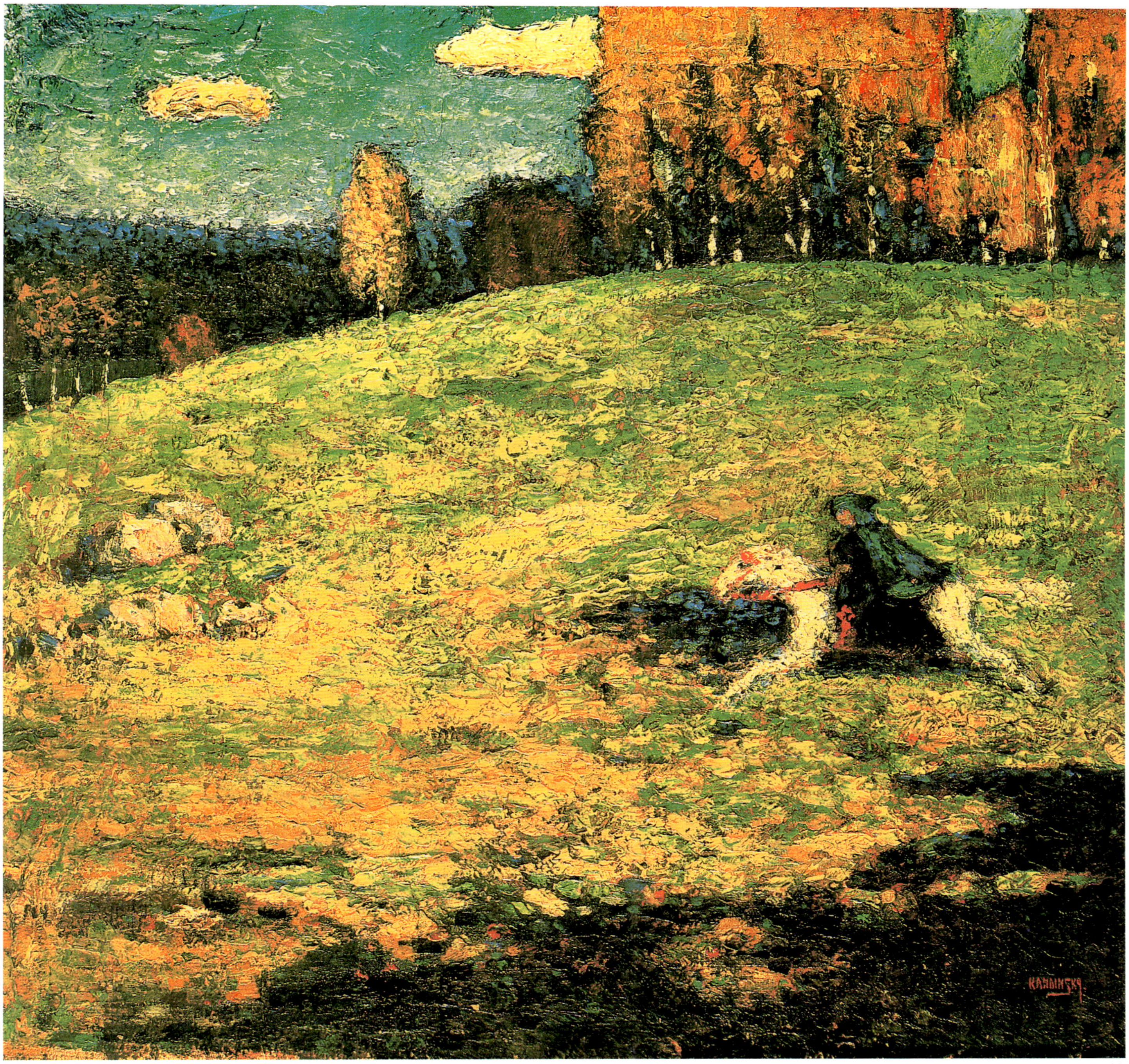

11

12

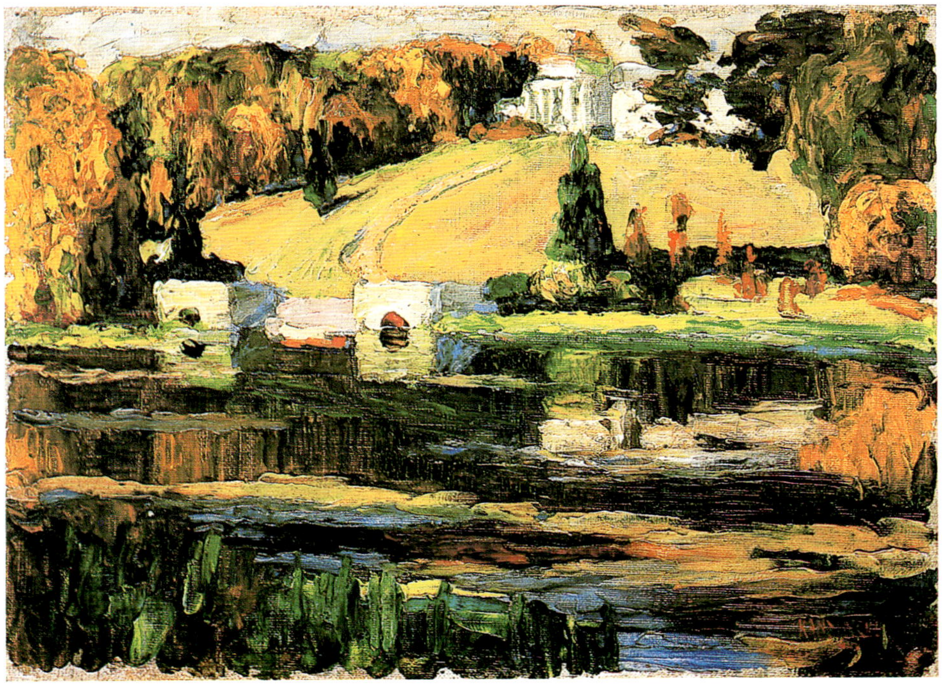

11 The Blue Rider, *1903. At this very early date, Kandinsky introduced what would become the emblem of the most famous of the several groups that he belonged to in his career. For the artist, blue was a celestial symbol; he equated this spiritual rider with the mythical St. George, defeating the "dragon" of materialism. His mysterious presence in the landscape, bathed in an eerie raking light, evokes the atmosphere of German folktales.*

12 *Sketch for* Achtyrka: Autumn, *1901. One of Kandinsky's earliest known works attests to the artist's familiarity with Symbolist painting, although its execution also betrays the influence of the French Impressionists, which began while he was still in Russia.*

13 Riding Couple, *1906–7. The ornamental quality of Kandinsky's early pointillism makes it not unlike the work of Gustav Klimt, and, like that Viennese artist, Kandinsky here explores the decorative aspects of painting as they relate to architectural design. Though the subject suggests a Russian folktale, it is depicted against the transfigured silhouette of an imaginary Moscow—a magical skyline of gilded domes—on the opposite bank of the river.*

13

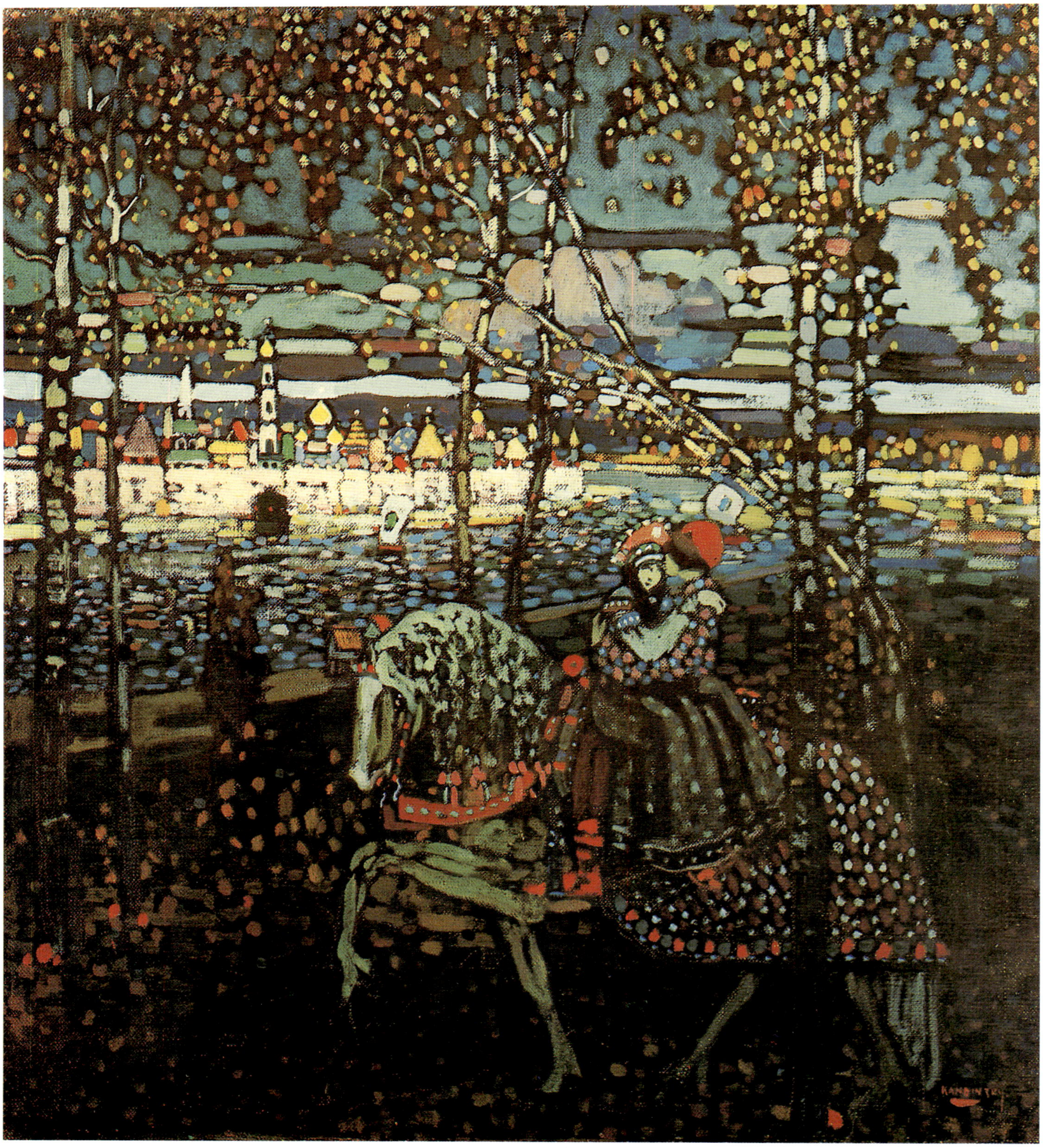

14

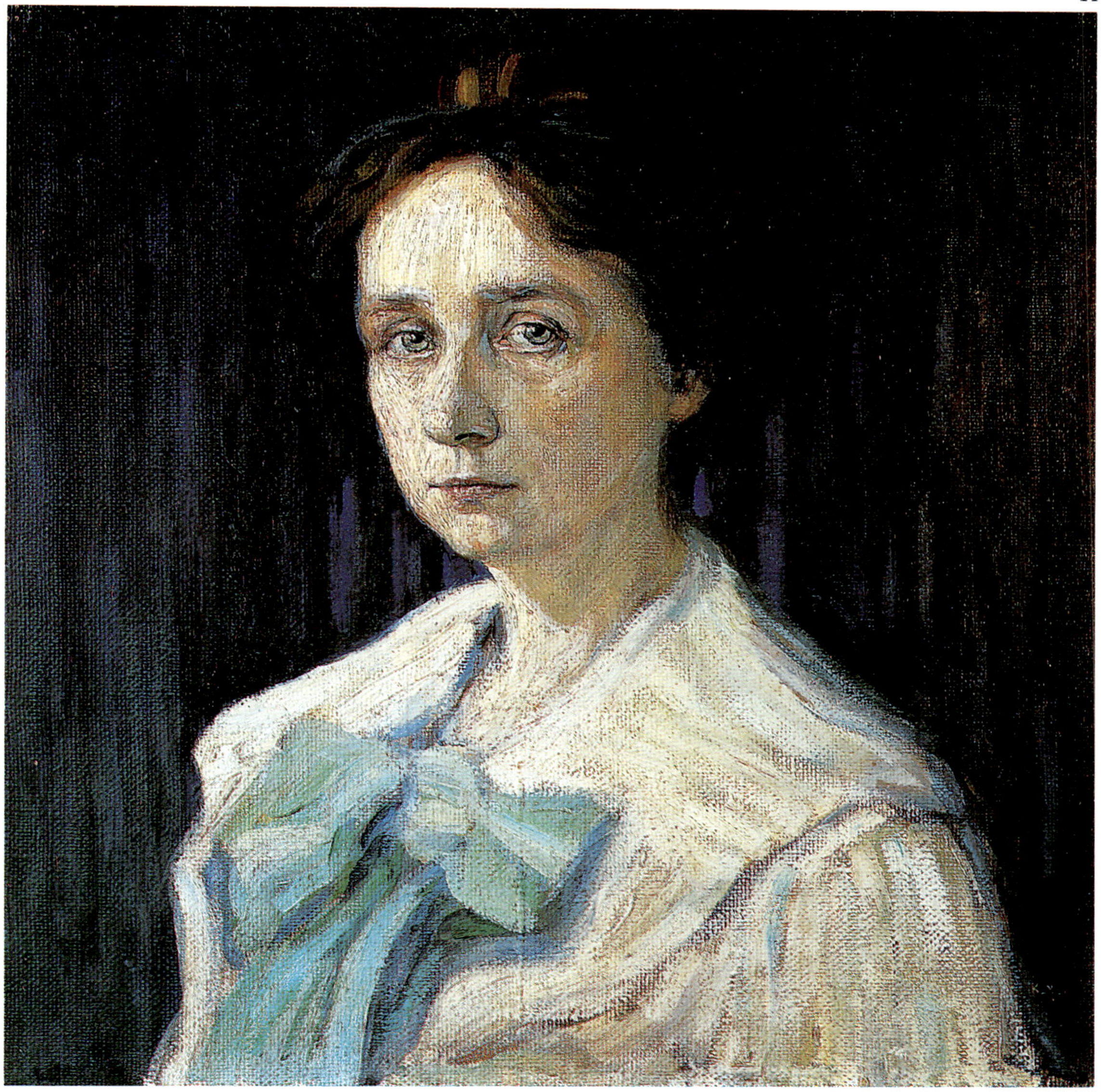

15

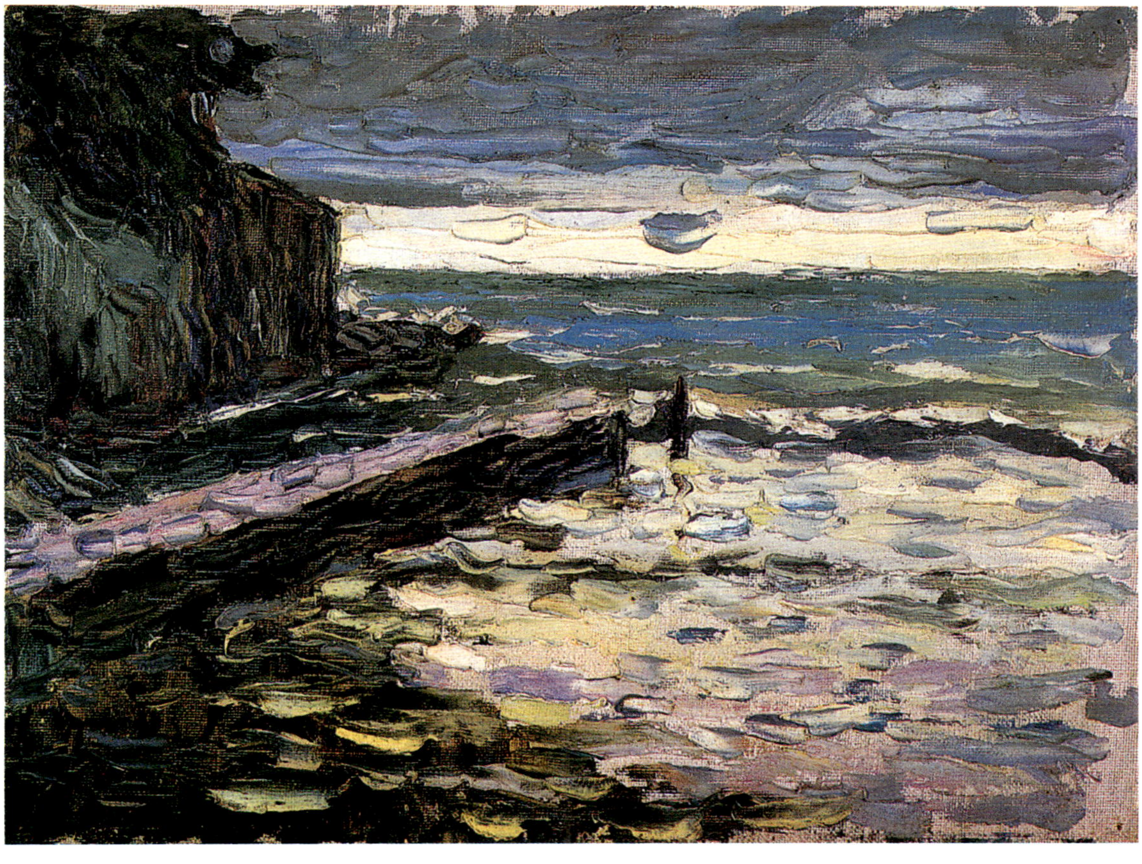

14 Portrait of Gabriele Münter, *1905. The Phalanx group operated an art school, where Kandinsky met Gabriele Münter, a young German painter who shared his life until 1914. In Moscow, Kandinsky had been married to his cousin, Anna Chemiakina, from whom he was amicably divorced in 1911, when his relationship with Münter was already long established. Münter's sensitive, intelligent features appear in several portraits that Kandinsky painted in those years.*

15 Rapallo: Rough Sea, *1906. This picture was painted in Italy, where Kandinsky was traveling with Münter. The technique suggests Monet, but the atmosphere of mystery and melancholy belongs entirely to the Romantic traditions of Northern Europe.*

16

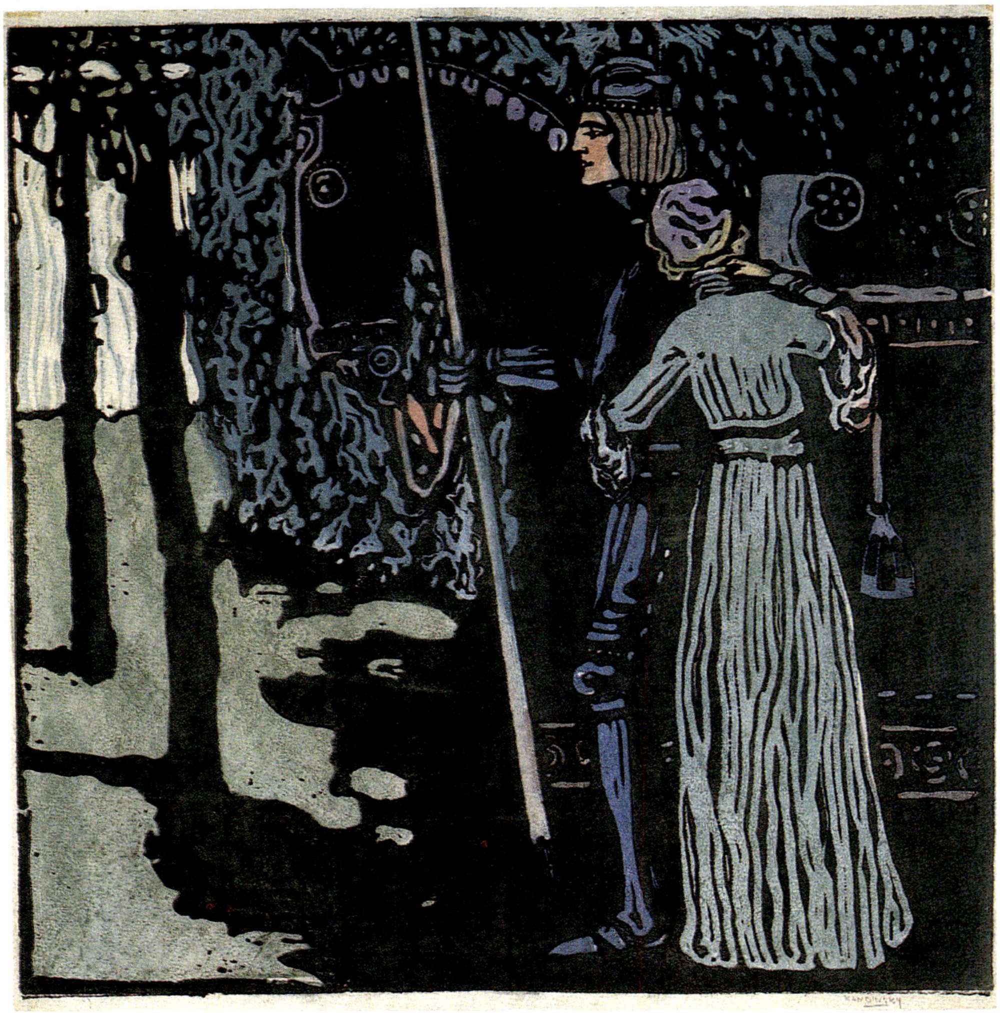

16 The Farewell, *1903. During his first years in Munich, Kandinsky produced more woodcuts than oil paintings. This printmaking technique had been deeply rooted in German tradition since the late Middle Ages, and at the beginning of the twentieth century it was revived by artists of many different persuasions. Both the legendary subject of this work and Kandinsky's linear and decorative draftsmanship are clearly related to the woodcut tradition.*

17

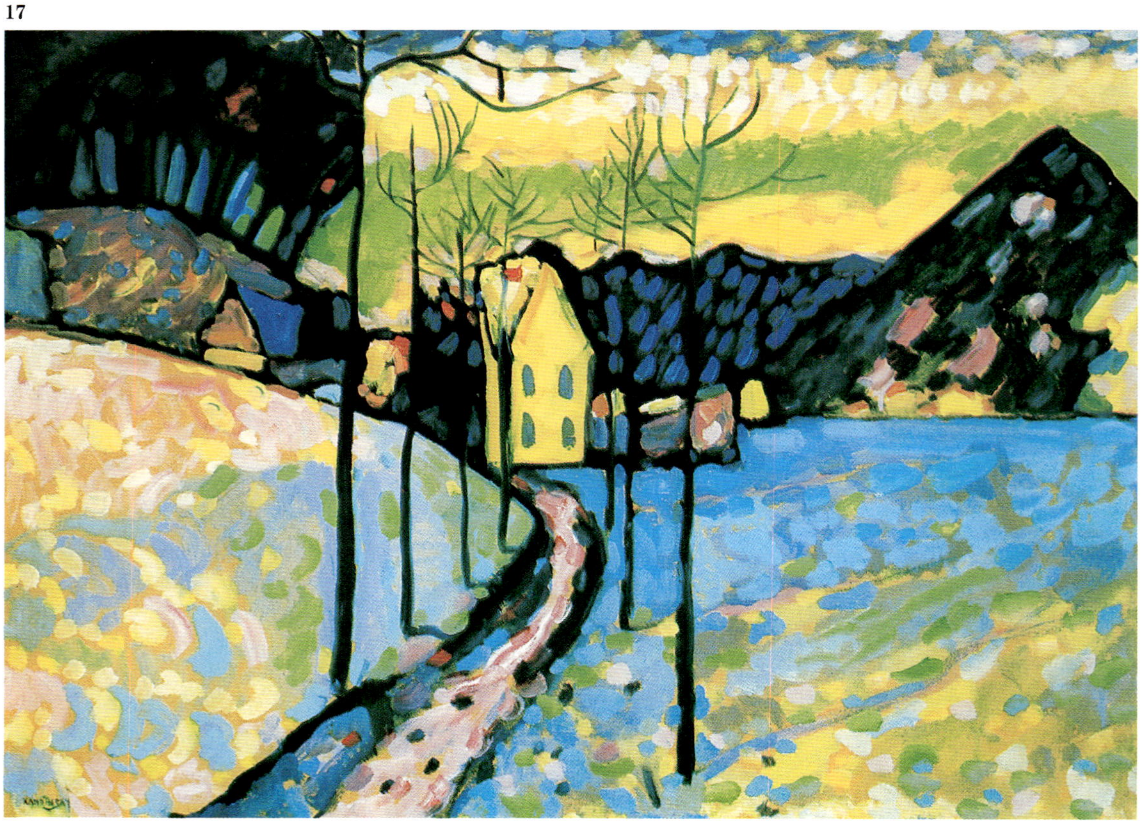

17 Winter Landscape I, *1909. The unexpected use of the color yellow, in the sky and on the house at the center of the composition, competes with the blue hues elsewhere in the landscape. This kind of opposition gives the painting an unsettling effect reminiscent of certain pictures that the Norwegian artist Edvard Munch was painting at about the same time.*

18 Blue Mountain, *1908–9. This image of horseback riders before a towering blue mountain—a color symbolizing the spiritual—is clearly allegorical. The blue-red-yellow triad constitutes one of the basic chromatic harmonies of Kandinsky's work in these years.*

18

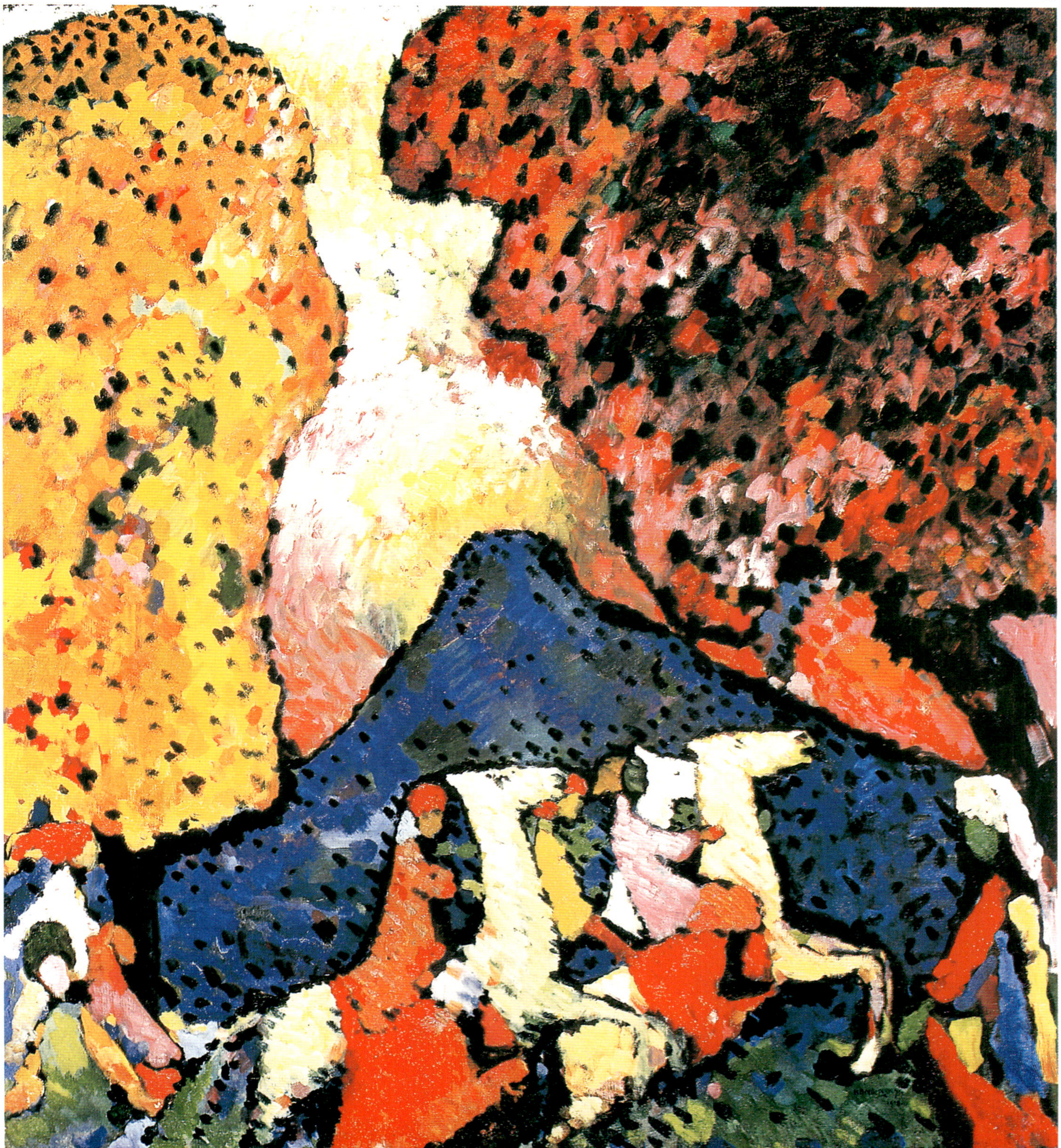

Abandoning Representation

The period from 1908 to 1910 was a personally rewarding one for Kandinsky, as reflected in the remarkable artistic progress of those years. With Gabriele Münter, he bought a house in Murnau, where he was able to spend long periods painting. Until at least 1912, recognizable objects continued to appear in some of his works, but the move to abstraction had already been made. The motif was increasingly dissolved into expanses of color, although he said that as yet he dared not discard it entirely for fear of falling into a merely decorative mode, or producing paintings "that resemble, to say it crudely, carpets or neckties. The beauty of color and form is not enough of a goal for art." He therefore sought to endow painting with spiritual values comparable to those he found in music. It was then that Kandinsky began calling his works Improvisations and Compositions, as though they were musical pieces.

19 Murnau: The Garden I, *1910. The ostensible subject is merely a pretext for the painter to weave a pattern of green, yellow, and red, augmenting that color chord with touches of blue and brown.*

20 Murnau: View with Railroad and Castle, *1909. The flattening of depicted objects, turning them into silhouettes, recalls the woodcuts that Kandinsky made during his first years in Munich.*

21 *Study for* Winter II, *1910–11. A complex area of yellows makes up the central triangle of pictorial space, and into it red and blue objects seem to sink as if in a fluid. The other triangular areas, above and below, create a sense of recession.*

19

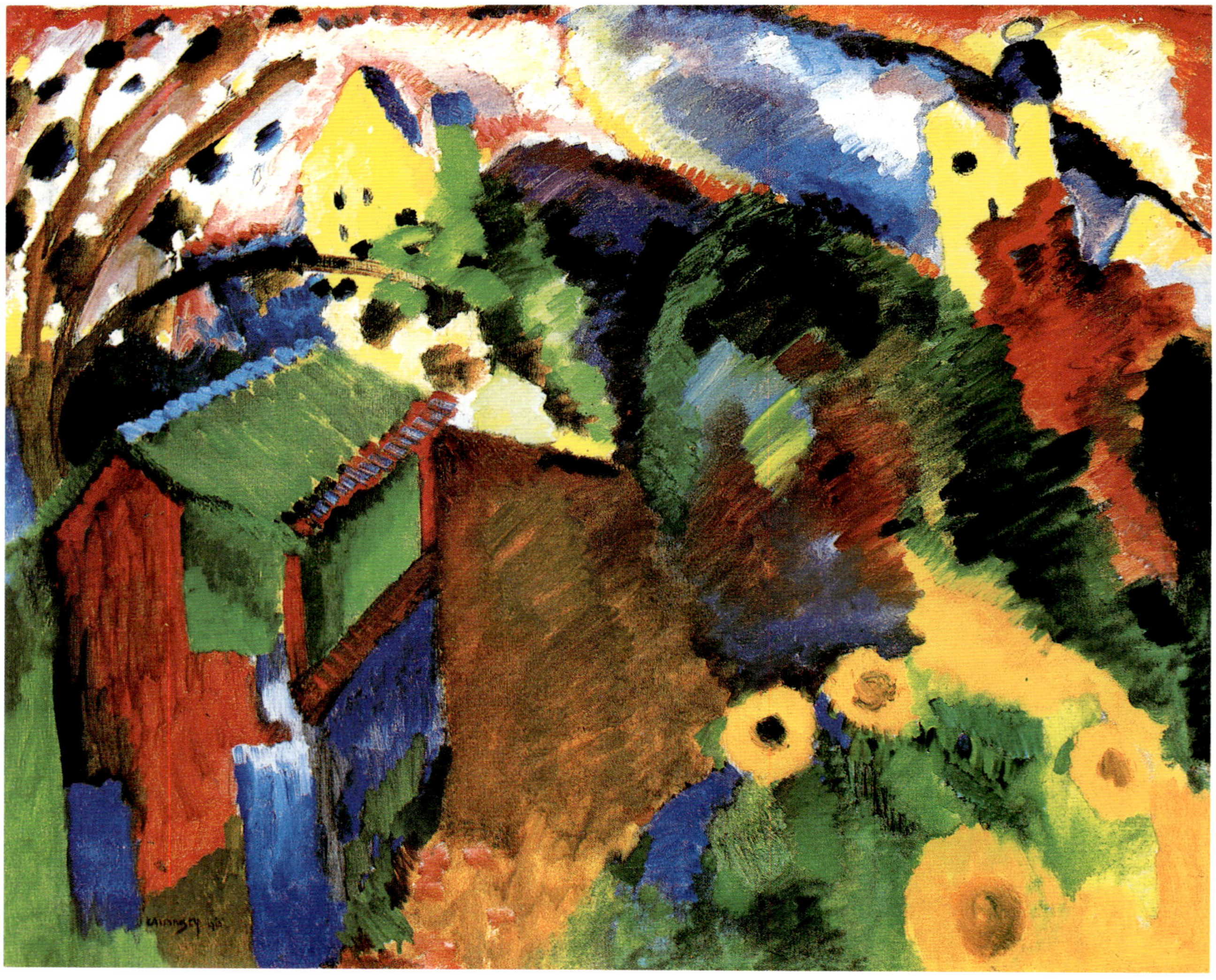

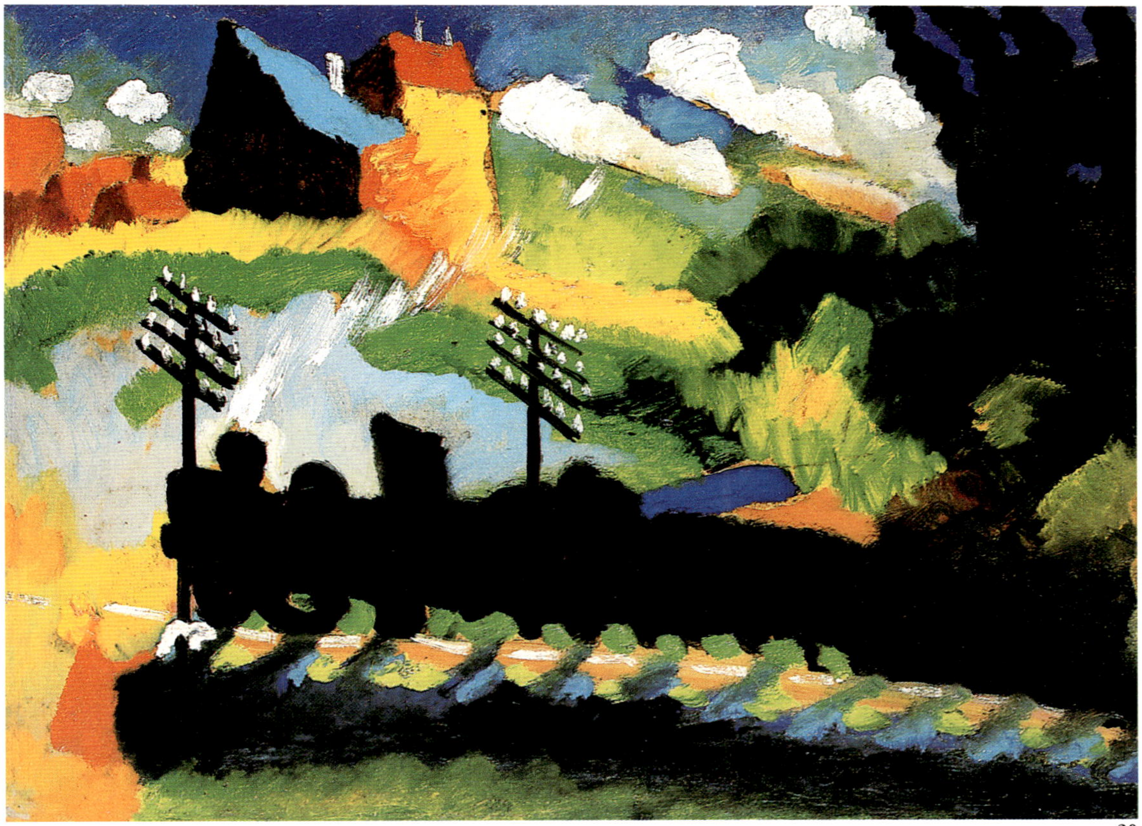

20

21

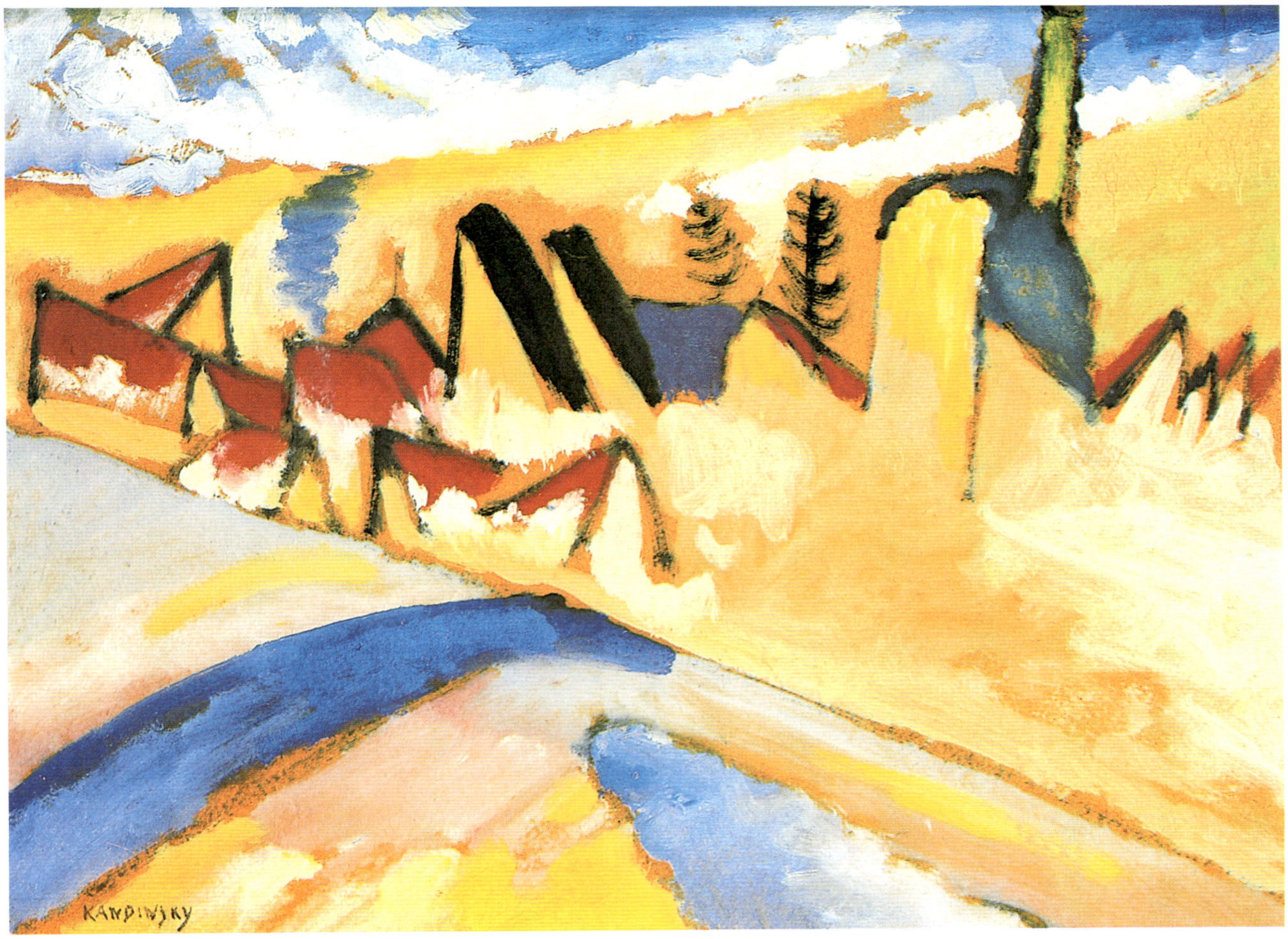

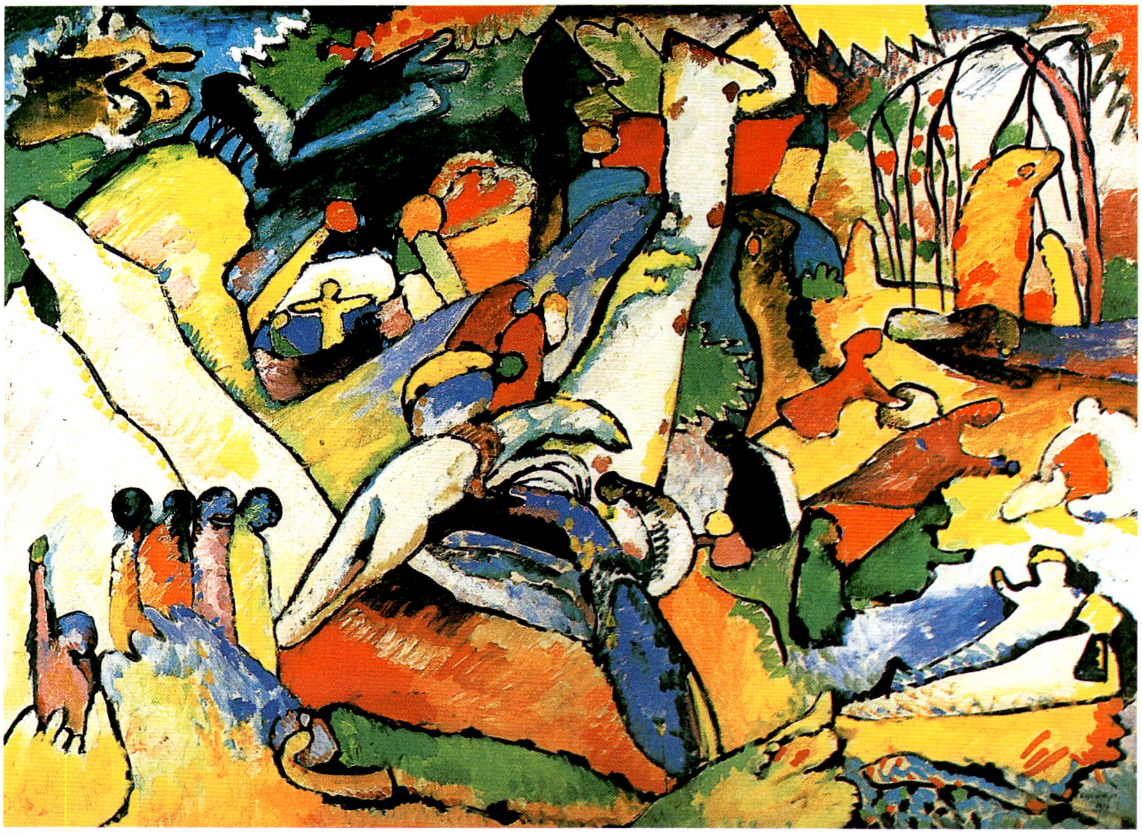

22

23

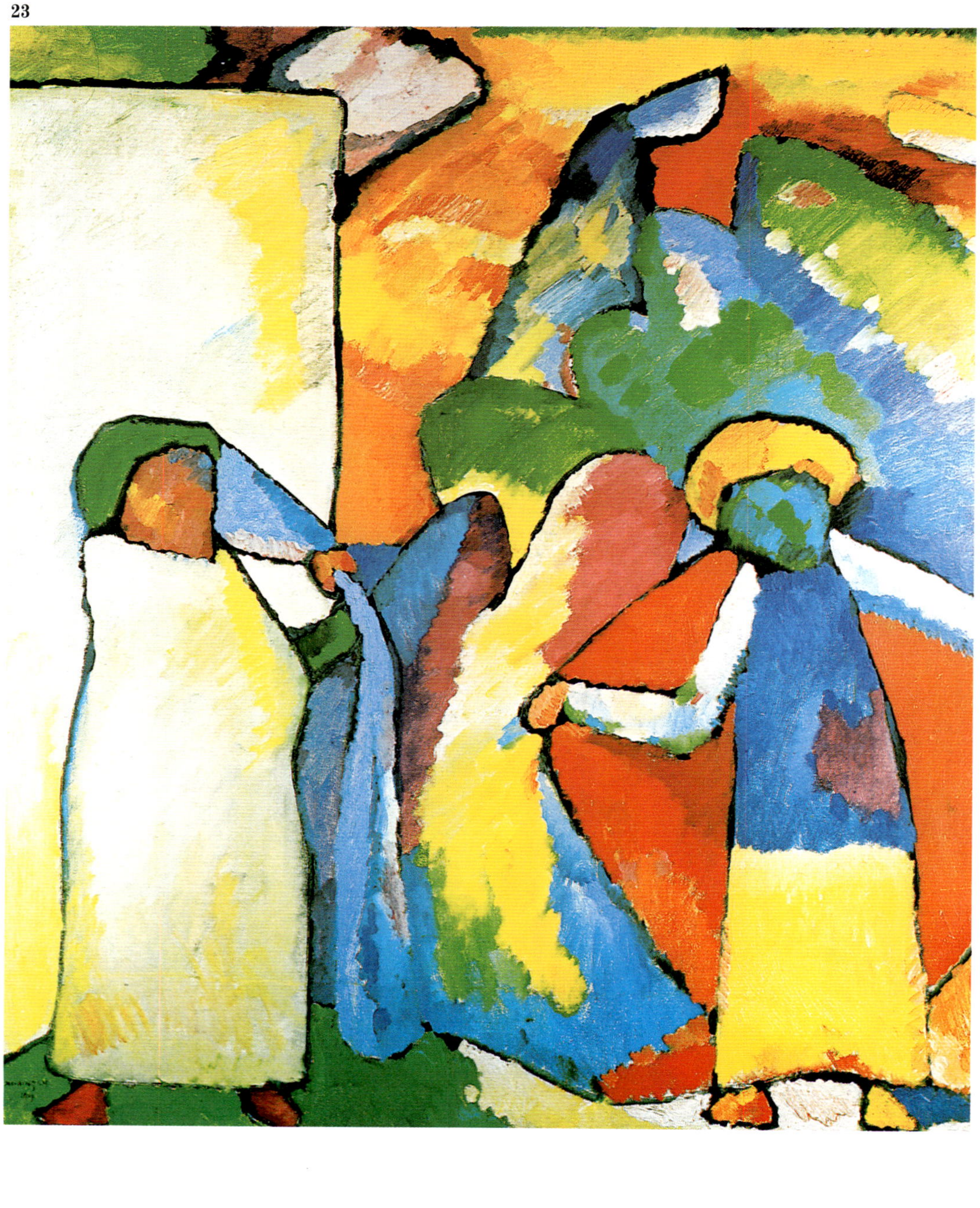

22 *Sketch for* Composition II, *1910. The final version of this work, Kandinsky's most ambitious up to that time, was lost in World War II. Shortly after its completion, it was shown at the second NKVM exhibition, where it aroused controversy. The welter of seemingly unrelated figures, caught in a whirlpool of color, signals a crucial stage in the painter's artistic development, the beginning of the break with representation.*

23 Improvisation VI, *1909. Kandinsky had visited Tunis with Gabriele Münter, and echoes of that trip can be found in some works from the time. The subtitle "Africana" is sometimes affixed to this painting, in which Kandinsky incorporated his experience of North Africa into his quest for a new artistic idiom.*

24 Improvisation VII, *1910. Along with* Composition *II (see study, plate 22), this is one of the earliest paintings in which Kandinsky discarded representation. The color arrangement, with barely any delimiting linear structure, transforms pictorial space into a zone of chromatic turbulence, a vortex that spirals in to the upper right quadrant of the painting.*

24

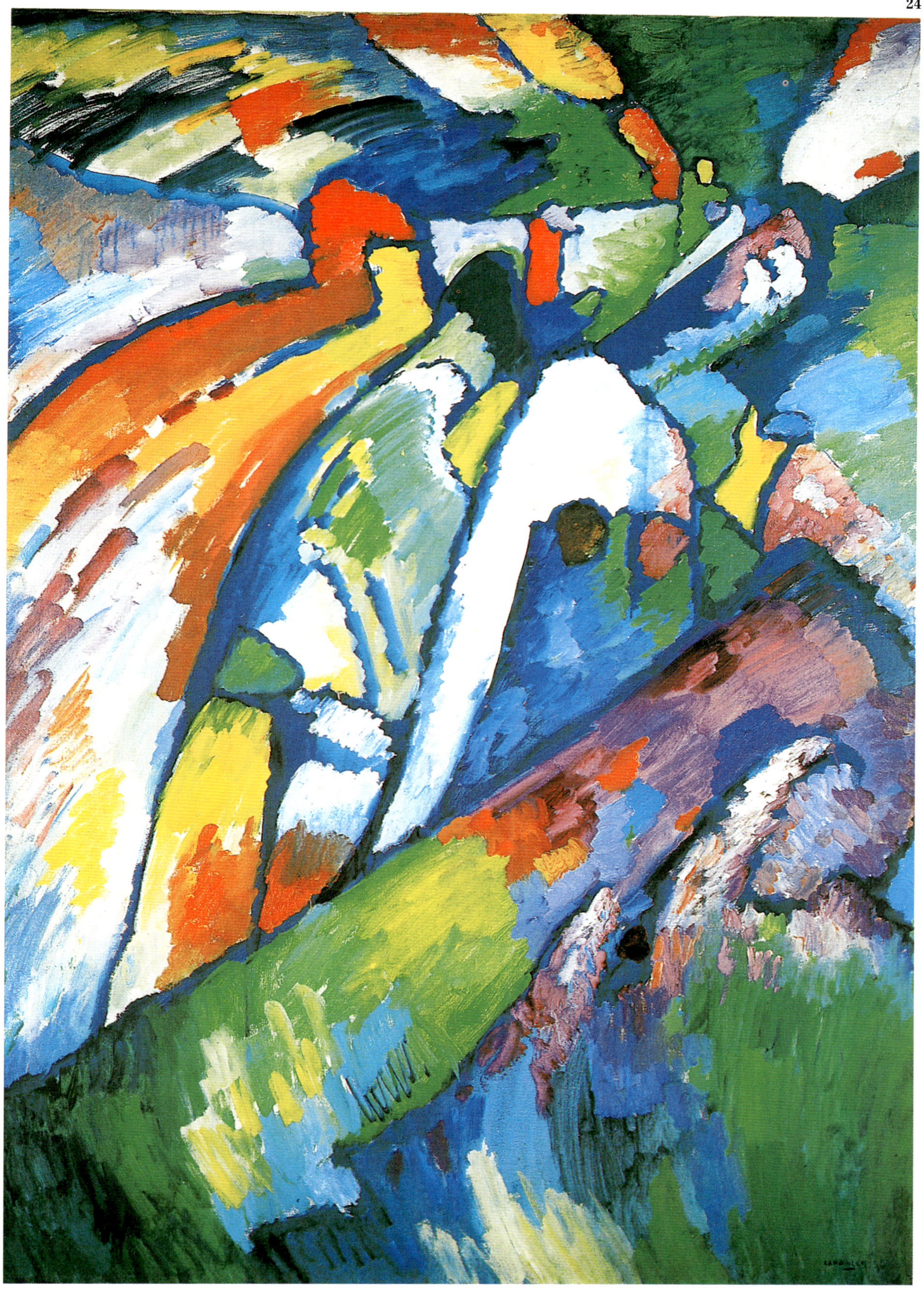

25

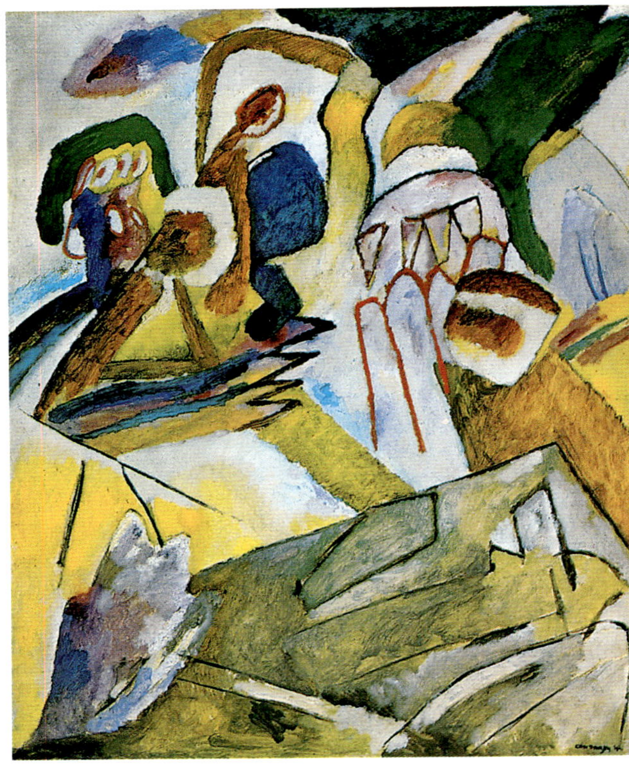

25 Improvisation XVIII (with Tombstones), *1911. The absence of hierarchical order in this painting is characteristic of the works of 1910 and 1911, as Kandinsky explored new territory.*

26 Improvisation XI, *1910. Vestigially representational elements can barely be identified here, having become almost ghostly. A bright yellow triangle is once again the center of attention of an entire composition.*

26

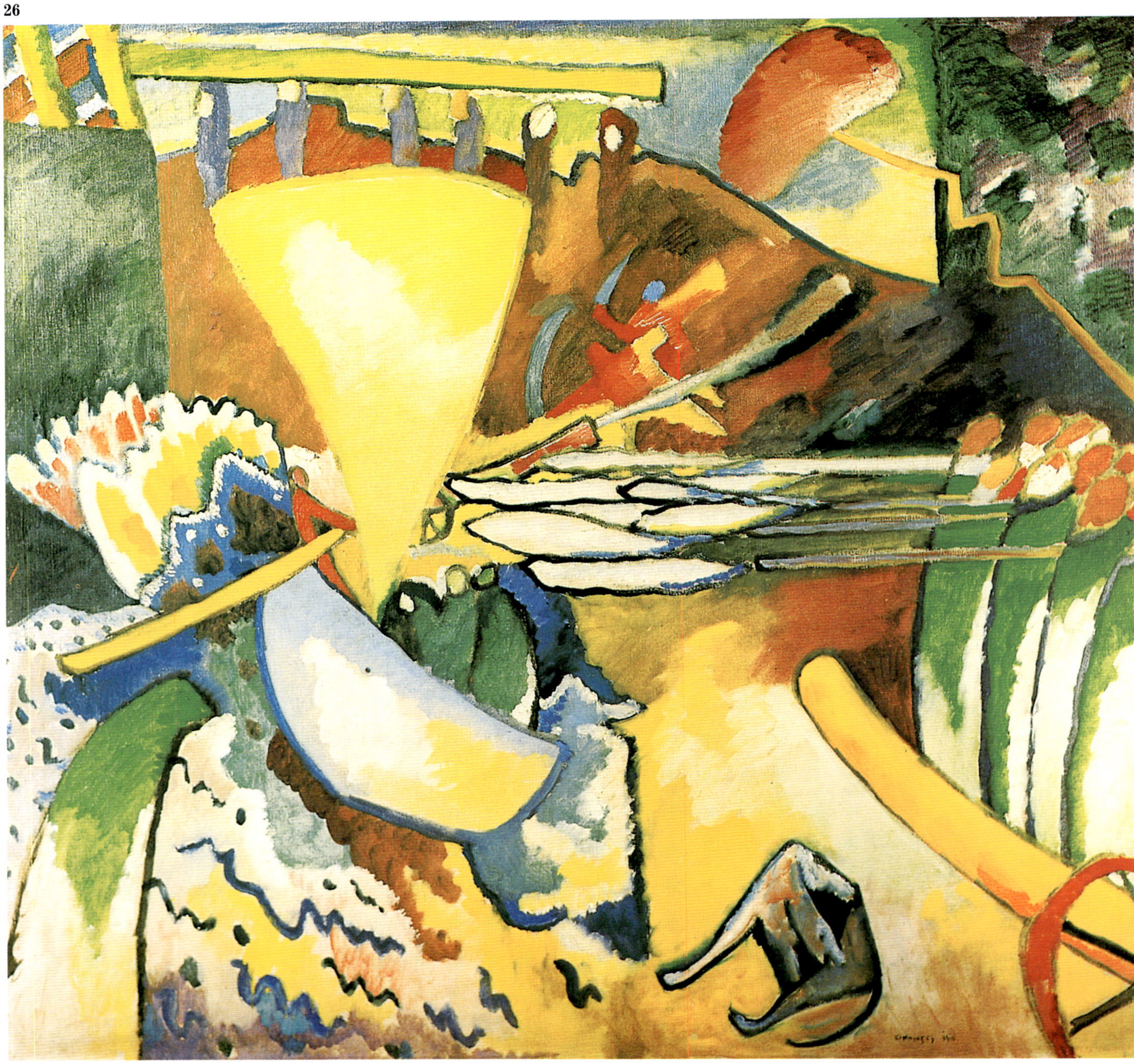

27 Passage by Boat, *1910. The subject of a boat with oarsmen appears frequently in these years, a time when Kandinsky thought of pure abstraction as a "voyage" to the terra incognita of a new world of painting. The oarsmen steer toward unknown waters, as the artist does; like him, they voyage from darkness to light.*

27

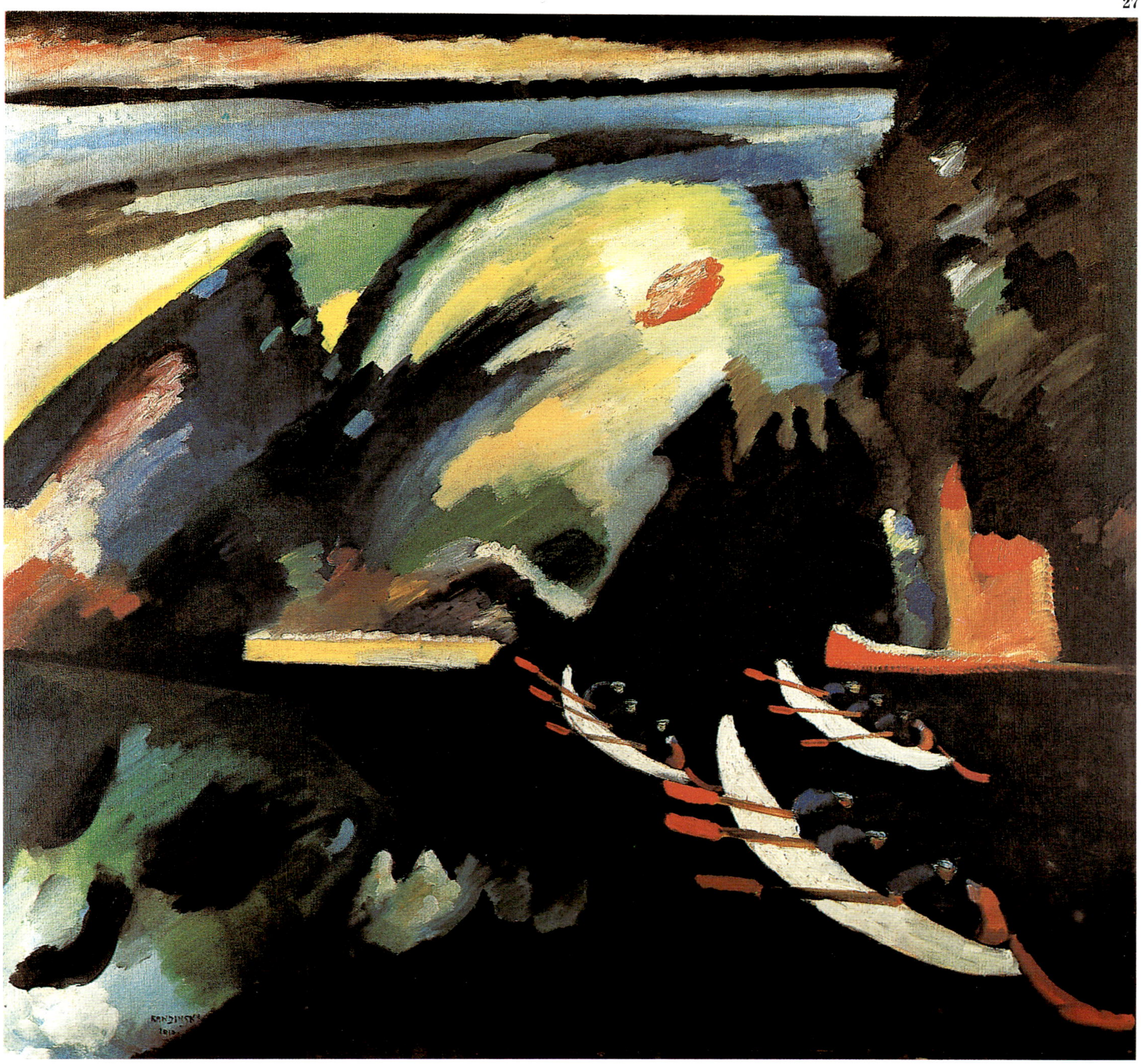

28 Improvisation XIX, *1911. The discontinuity between the figures, who are rendered with rough black brushstrokes, and the background of the painting—a broad, mottled area of variations on blue, and a warm, red border with touches of yellow and green—makes it possible to speak of color and line as two independent, almost unrelated structures. The harmony of the colors would be just as intelligible without the representational sketch: the insubstantial figures are hardly more than a way to emphasize the tension at the edges of the painting.*

29 All Saints' Day I, *1911. The same year, Kandinsky completed a representational version of this painting using a similar chromatic arrangement (see plate 47). In the present version, the areas of color intermingle in a maelstrom of directional tensions that establishes no clear hierarchical order.*

30 Autumn II, *1912. The tenuous diagonal across the lower portion of the painting gives rise to a spectacular image: a diaphanous landscape of soft, autumn hues is reflected in the still waters of a lake. In this case, it is the title that provides the key to the painting's colors, as elsewhere it is given by a reference to music.*

28

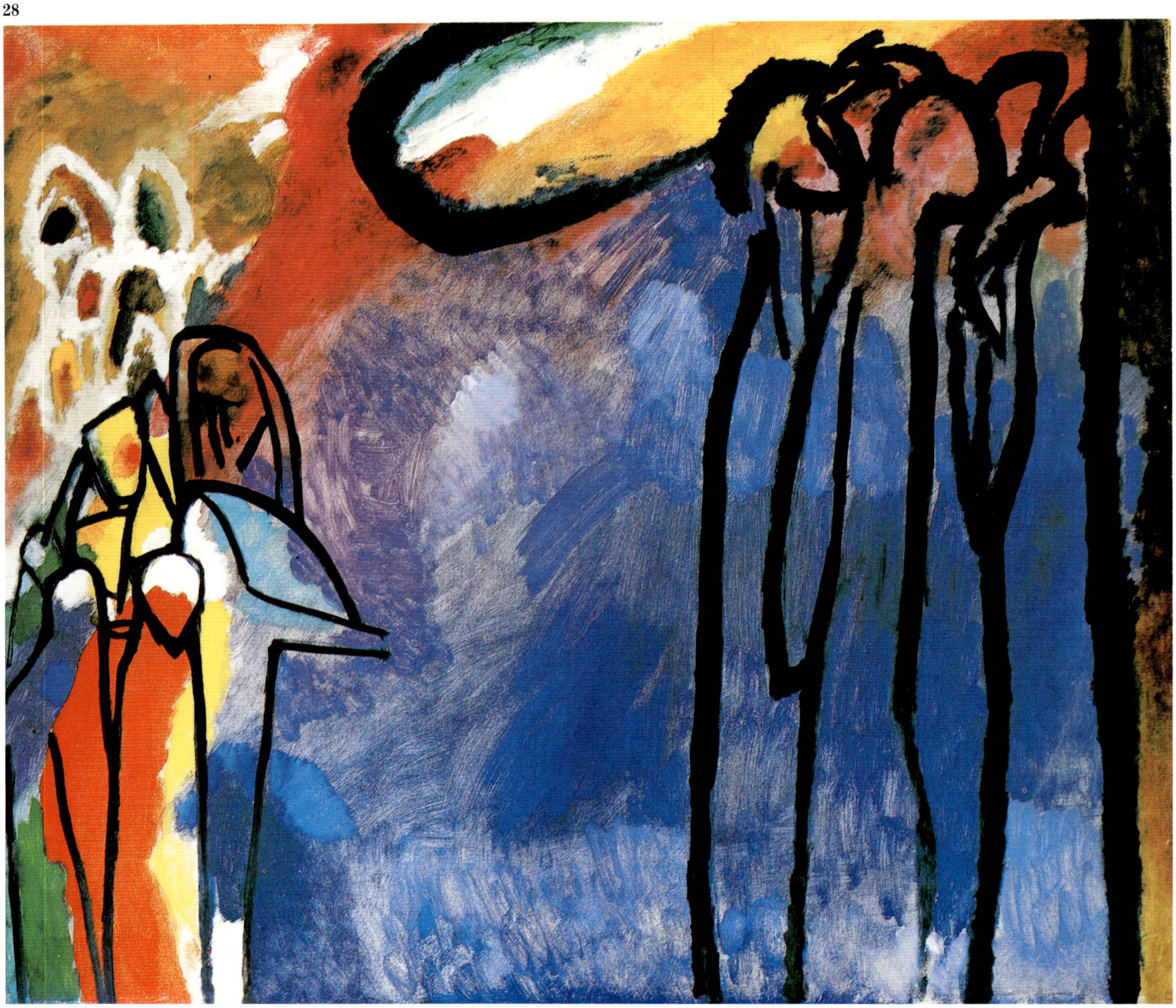

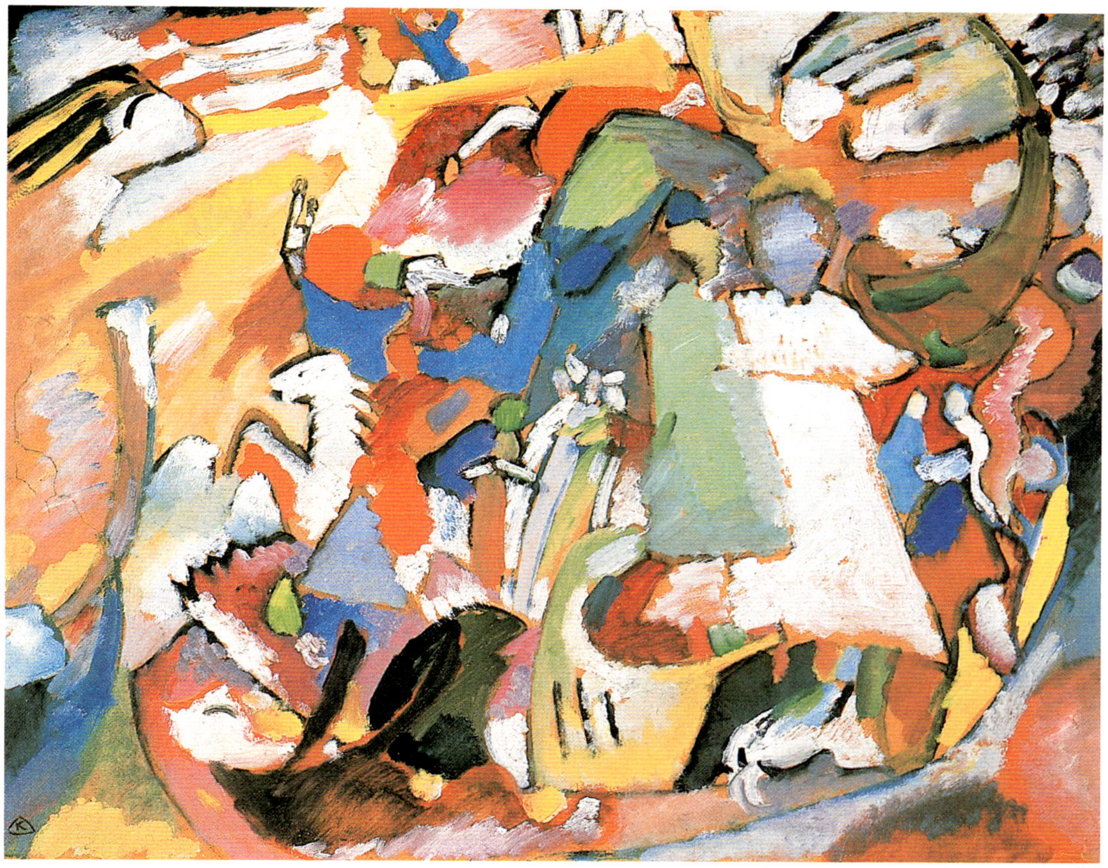

29

30

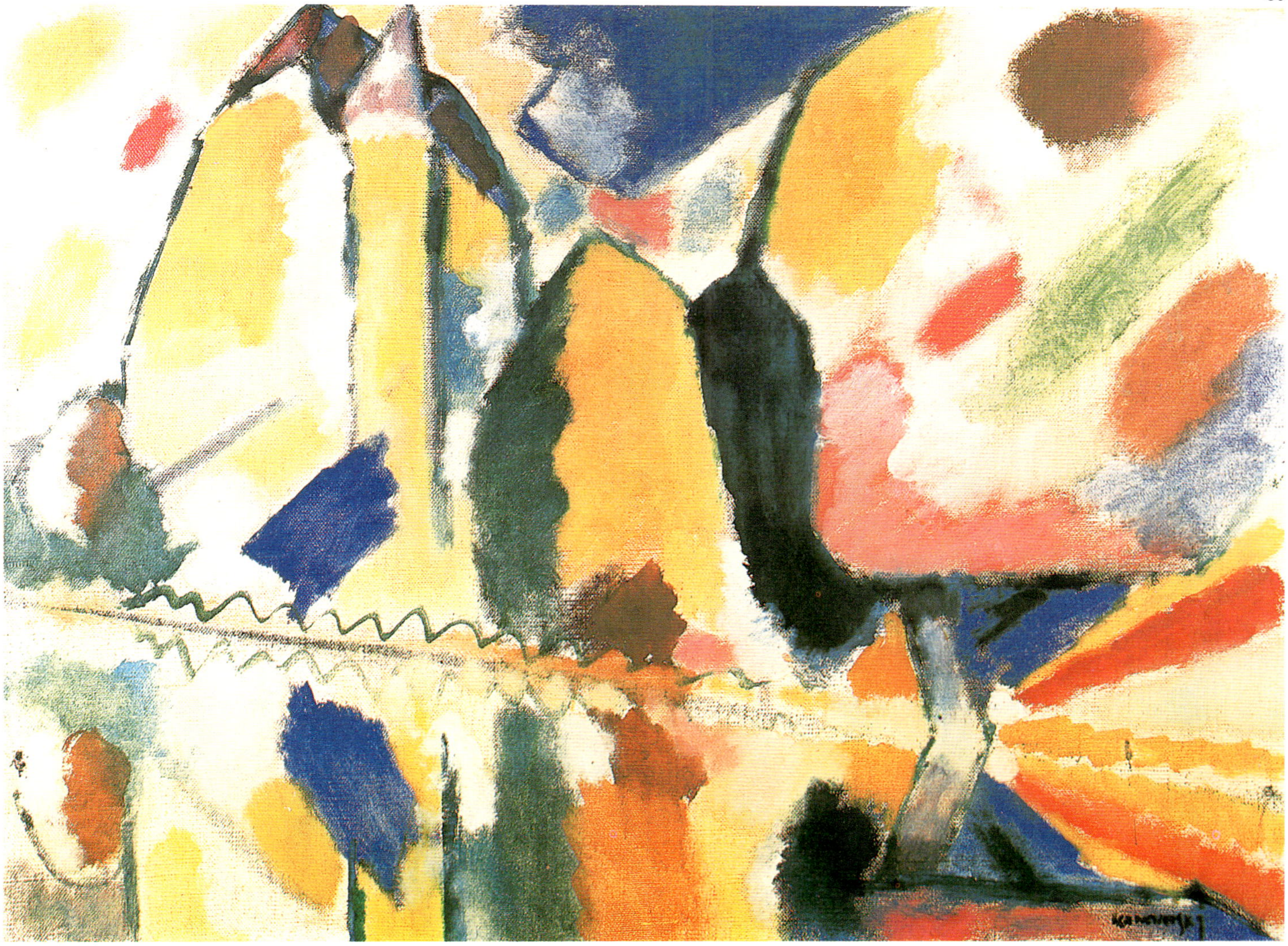

Non-Objective Painting

During the years from 1910 to the outbreak of World War I, Kandinsky created his own painterly domain. The openly nonrepresentational nature of his work caused tensions with the NKVM, which in 1911 refused to exhibit his *Composition V* (private collection), claiming that its format did not comply with the mandatory requirements of the association. But as a result, Kandinsky strengthened his friendships with Franz Marc and Arnold Schoenberg, which led to the forming of the Blue Rider. At the same time, Kandinsky pursued his interest in theosophy, which was to become a spiritual resource for his work as an artist. His paintings were already nonrepresentational; only a few spare brushstrokes occasionally still hinted at figures and objects, now more as oblique allusions to the painting's meaning than as its actual subject. Such vestiges of representation only served to demonstrate Kandinsky's awareness of his role as the founder of a new kind of painting: with their traces of such subjects as the Deluge, the Apocalypse, and the voyage to unknown waters, these works are all images of a great ending, but also of regeneration and of arrival in a new, reborn world. The theme of these paintings is not merely the conflict between vibrant masses of color but, as the artist said, "the perception of the spiritual in material and abstract things."

31 Composition IV, *1911. The rainbow that arches between the mountains establishes the basic color harmony, a blue, yellow, and green chord with strokes of red. The black lines are little more than a template laid over the areas of color.*

32 Improvisation XIII, *1910. Paintings like this one, in which representational content has dissolved into color, best exemplify Kandinsky's work during the years before World War I. Here, the masses of color are contained by thick black strokes that might as well be cast shadows.*

33 Impression V (Park), *1911. The black lines that constitute the figurative elements in this painting were developed from an observed motif, but they have little relation to the chord of primary colors that is the true essence of the work.*

31

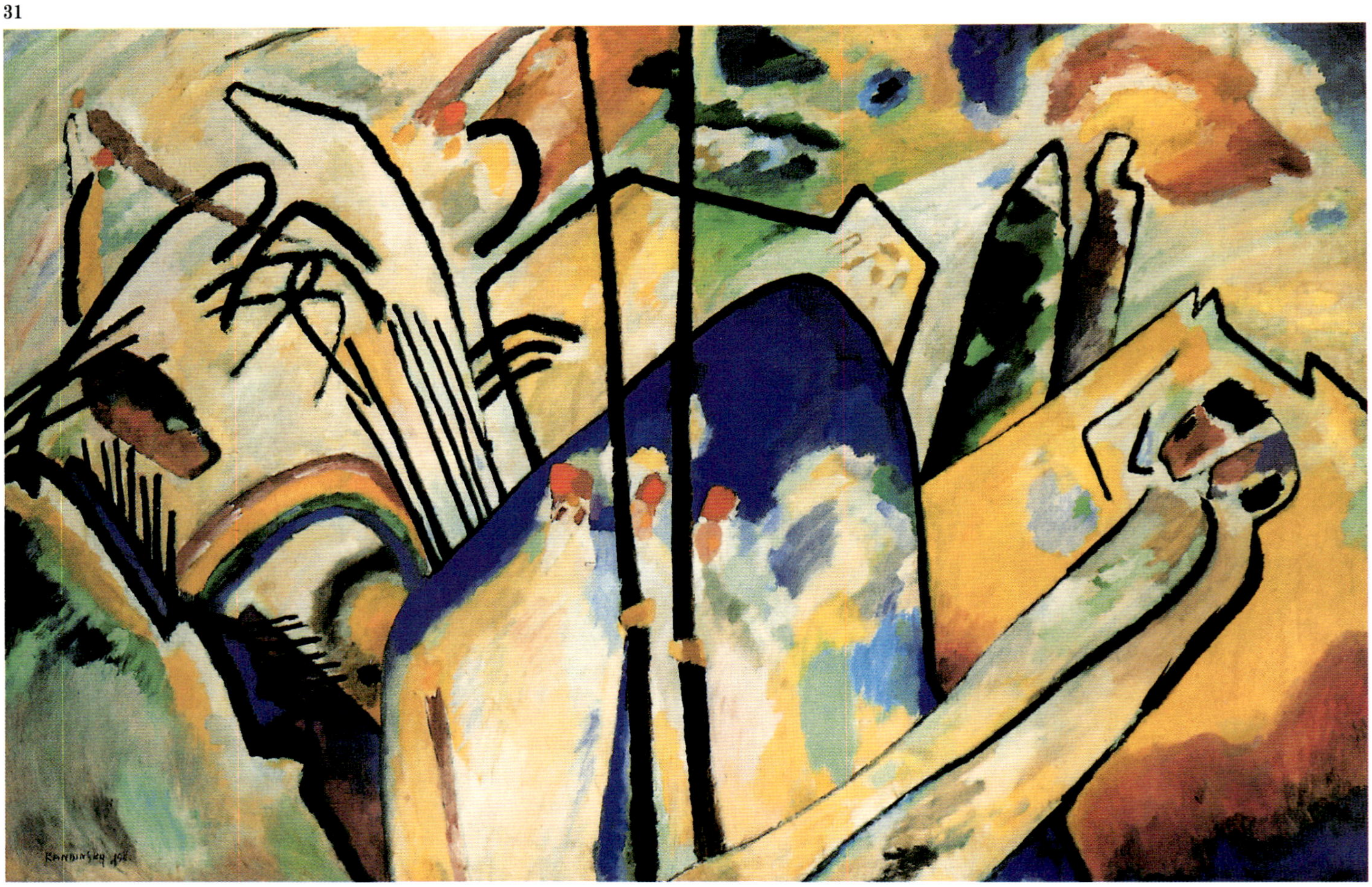

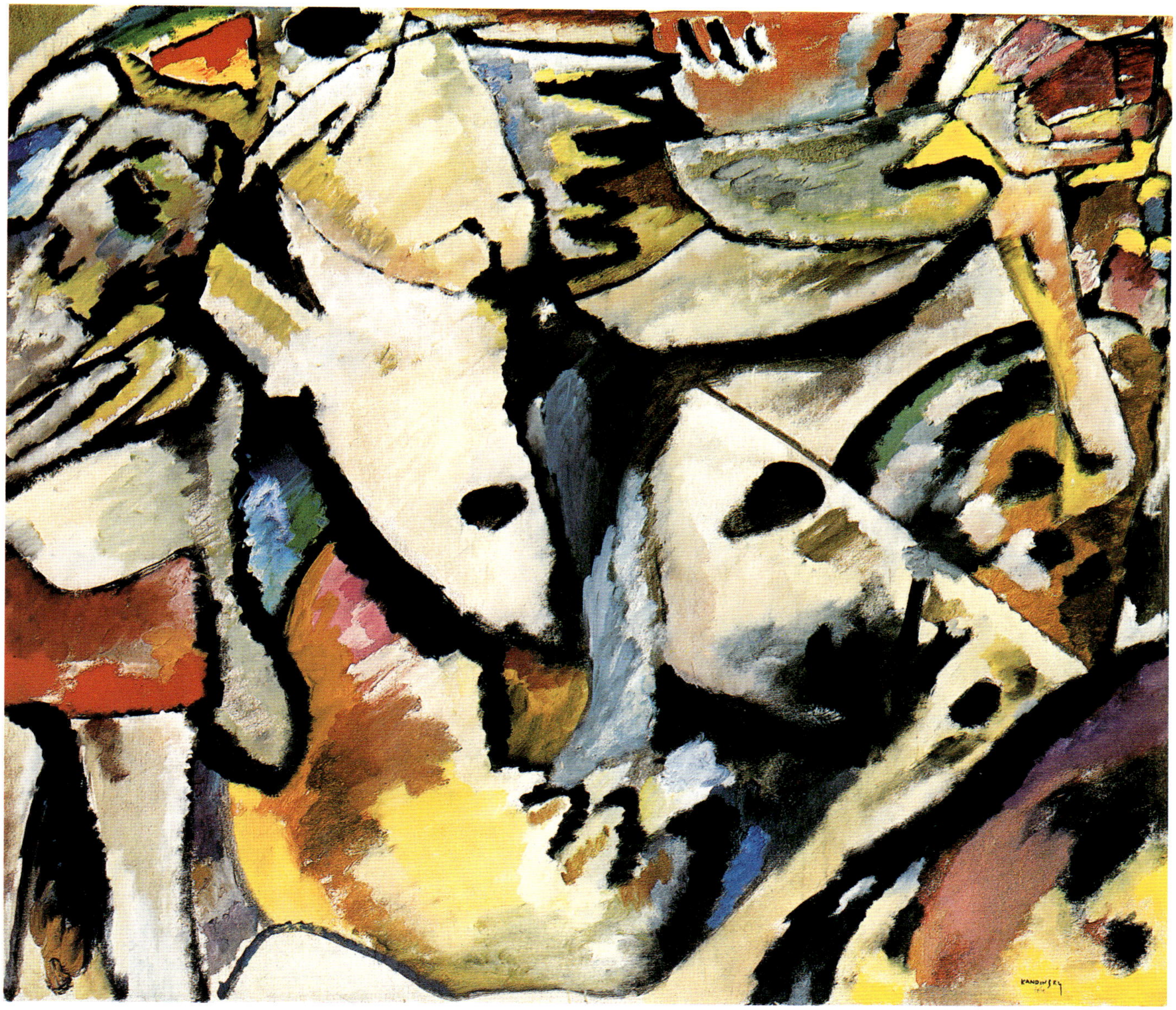

32

33

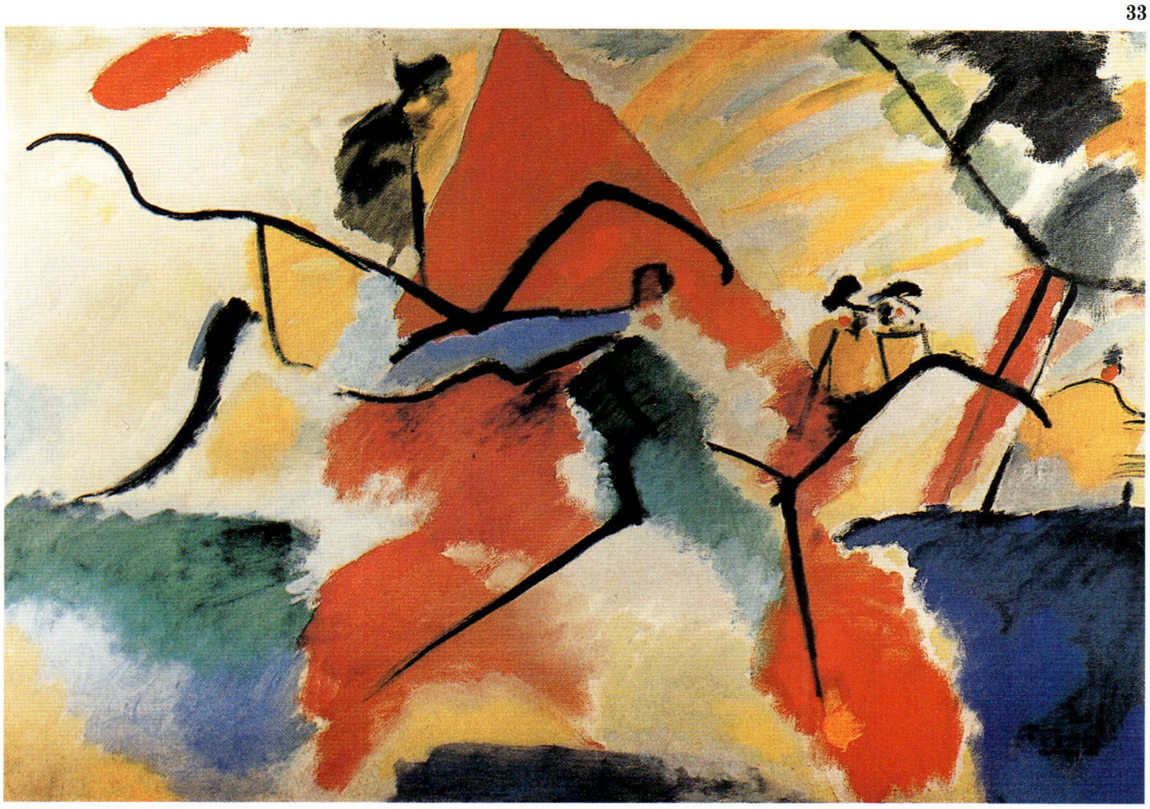

34 St. George II, *1911. Differently colored angular shapes cluster like vectors around a yellow diagonal. The organization of the painting is reminiscent of certain Cubist ideas of spatial structure; however, both the date of this work and the nature of Kandinsky's aesthetic decisions make it diffcult to imagine a direct influence.*

34

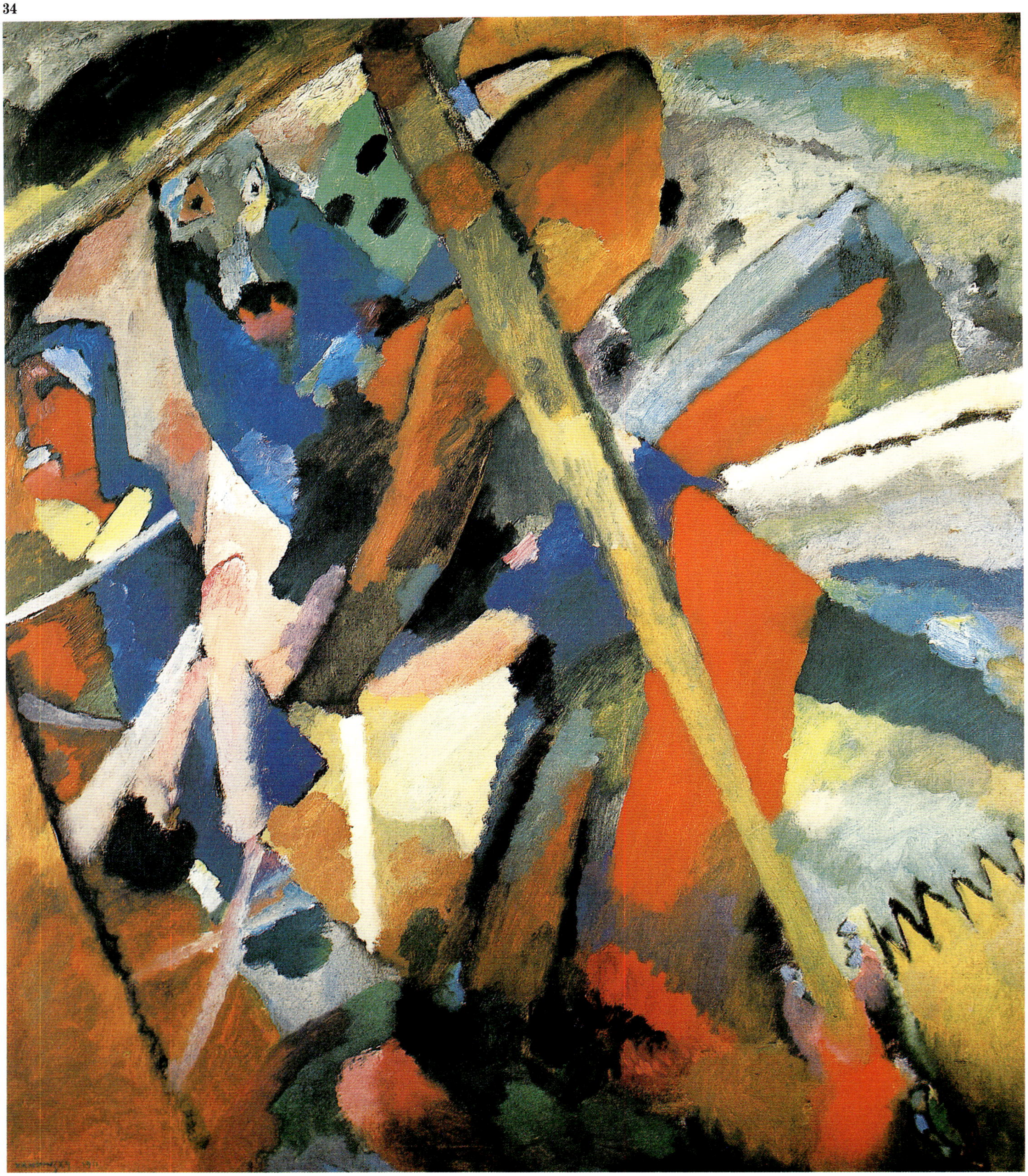

35

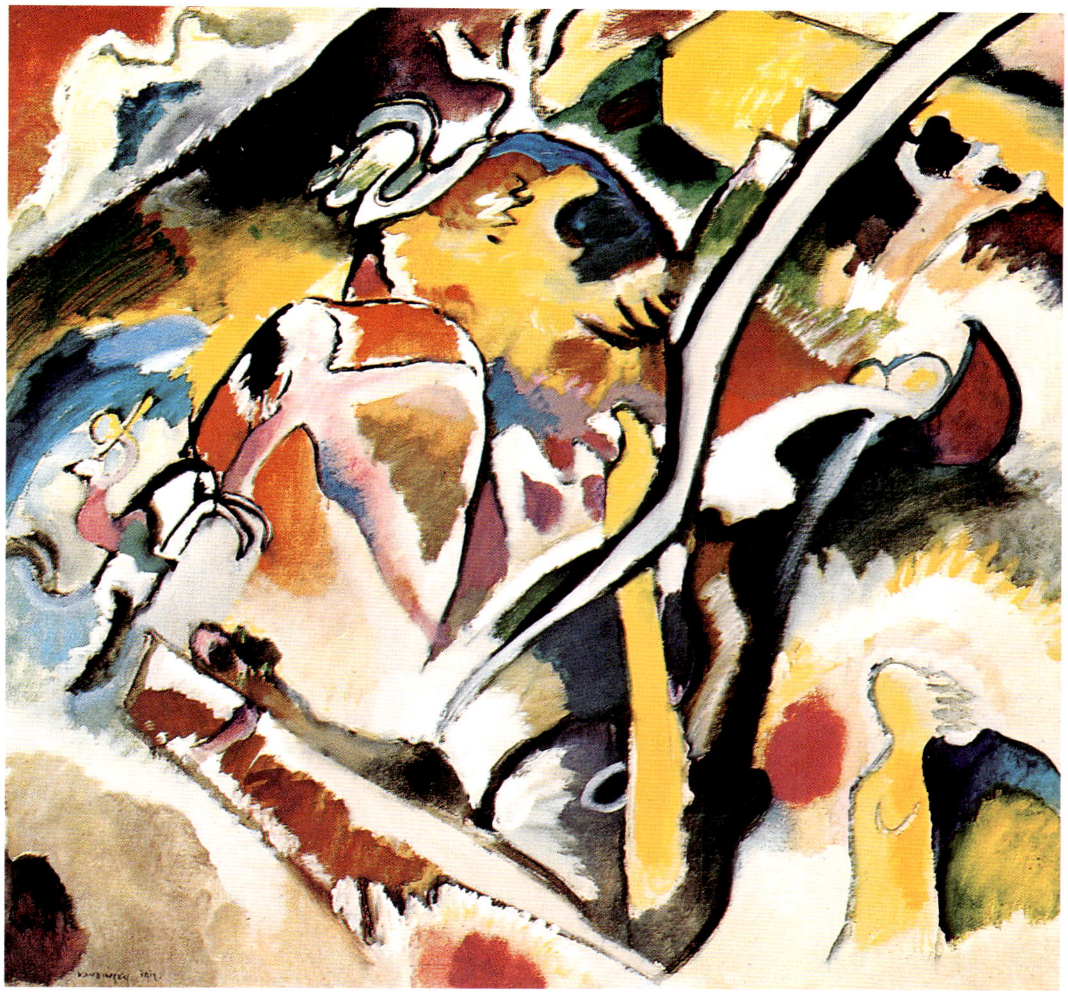

35 Deluge I, *1912. Kandinsky's allusion to the biblical Deluge is one of the most frequent metaphors of regeneration at this stage of his career. Here, a downpour of shapes tumbles through a range of colors, from the intense yellows to white to the reddish-greens at the back.*

36 Improvisation XXVIII *(second version), 1912. Kandinsky viewed the painterly process of the Blue Rider years as a way of freeing the spiritual from the world of matter. This may explain the chaotic appearance of certain works, where the artist seems to be releasing powerful forces that he cannot as yet control.*

36

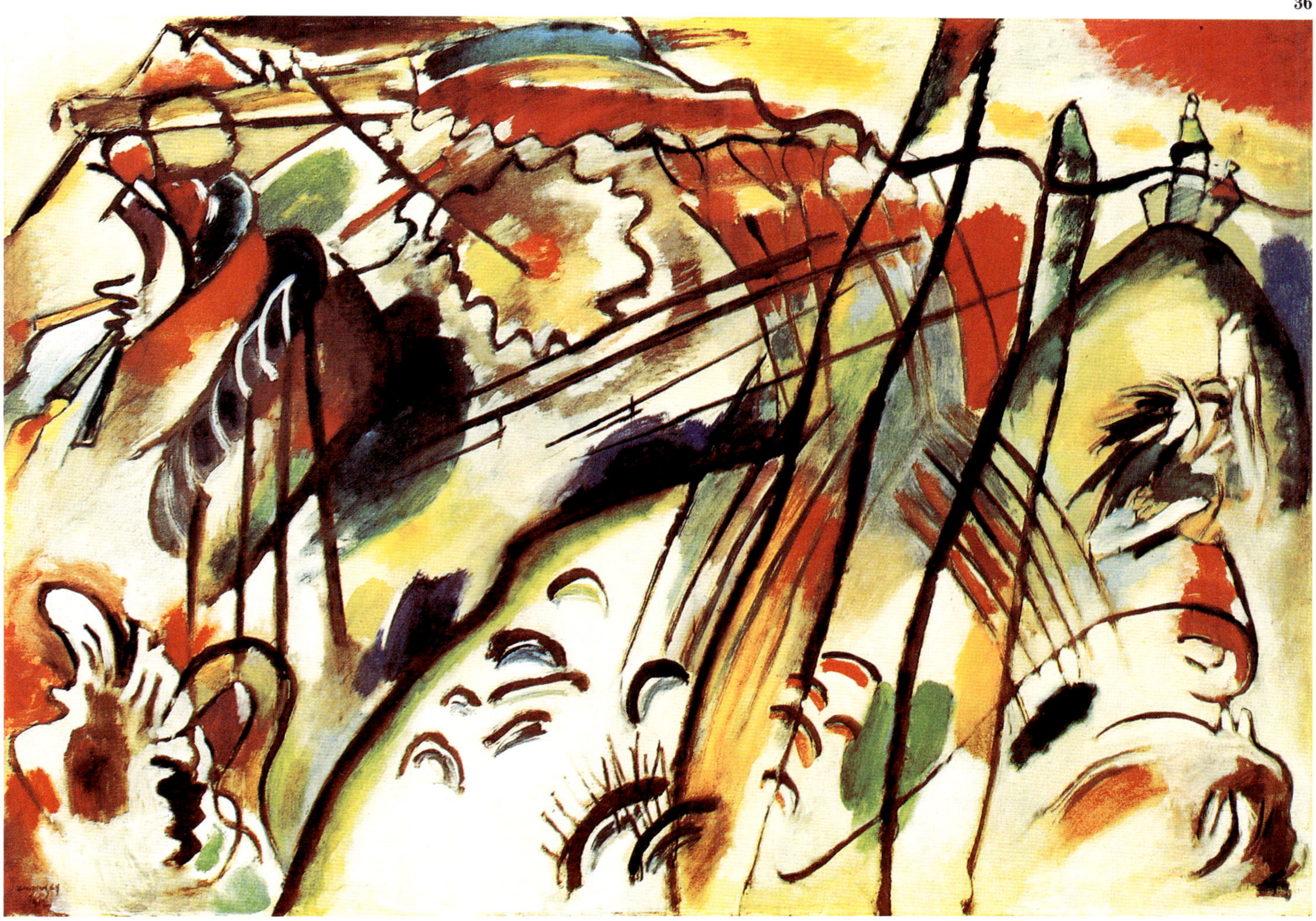

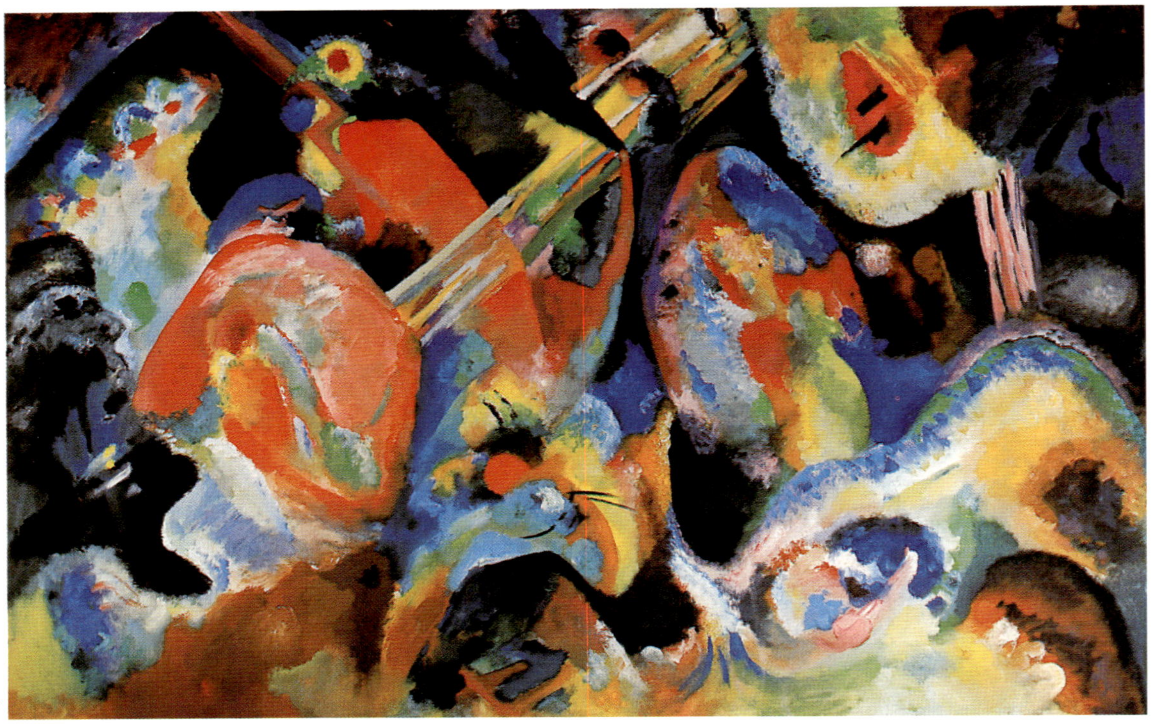
37

38
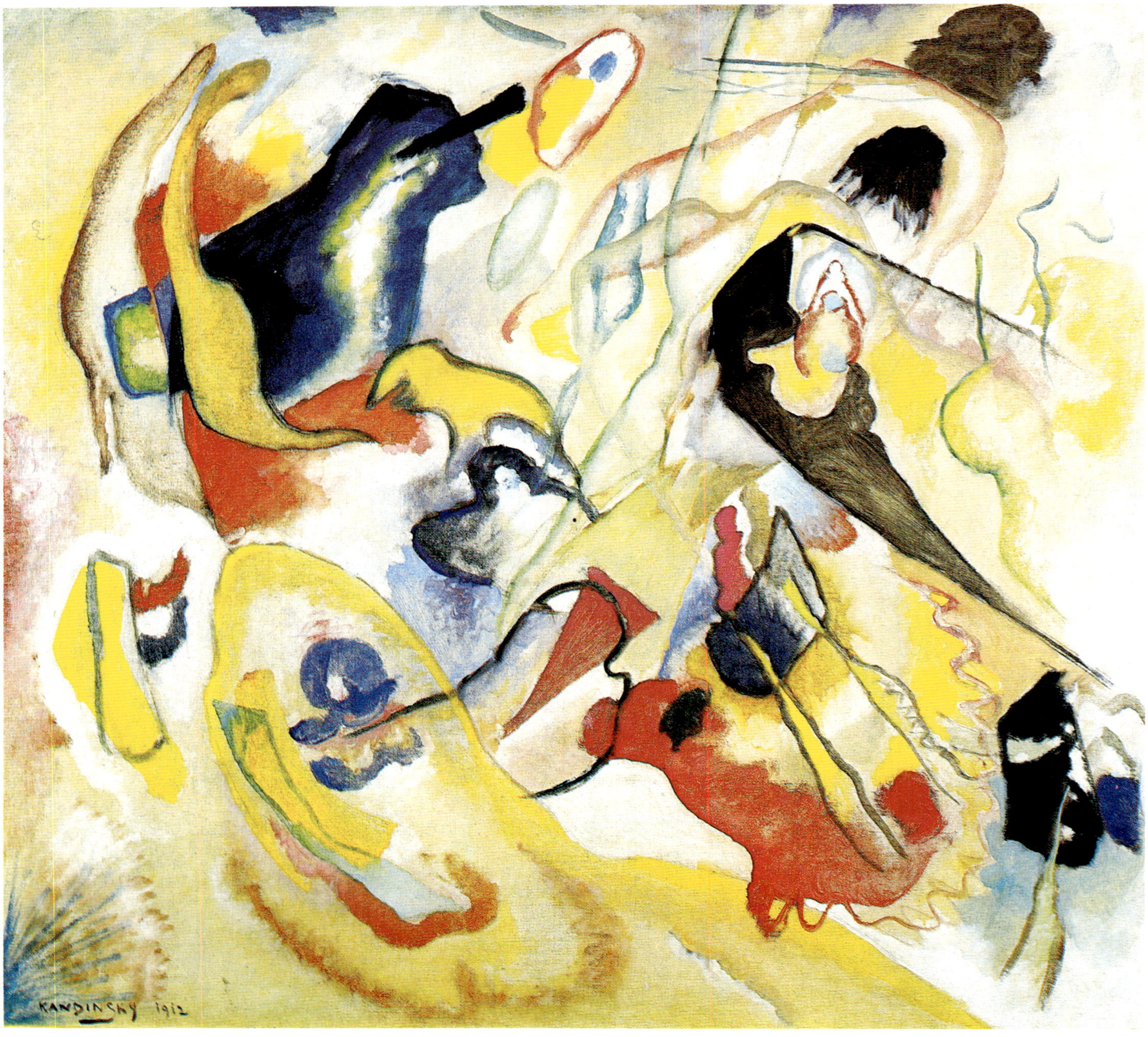

37 Improvisation (Deluge), *1913. Once again, Kandinsky alludes to the biblical Deluge and to the idea of chaos. Here, however, the relatively cool colors and the black background dampen the explosive energy of the scene, and Kandinsky lowers the temperature of the large red shapes by putting layers of calmer colors on top of them. The three rays across the upper part of the painting suggest the symbolic oars in the works that he painted in 1910 (see plate 27).*

38 *Study for* Deluge II, *1912. The entire composition responds to the diagonal current that originates in the lower left corner. The warmest and most vibrant tones—yellows and reds—create the foreground, with blues and browns for the most part restricted to the top and right.*

39 Improvisation XXVI (Rowing), *1912. A wavy red line splits the pictorial surface into two unequal parts. Once again, rowing figures are defined by a few black strokes, here laid over the pattern of color areas. The black lines establish a forceful diagonal that gives the painting its dynamic quality, and they thus impose a certain tension on the more static background. By showing the tension between such wholly different elements, Kandinsky wanted to convey the opposition between the material and spiritual worlds.*

39

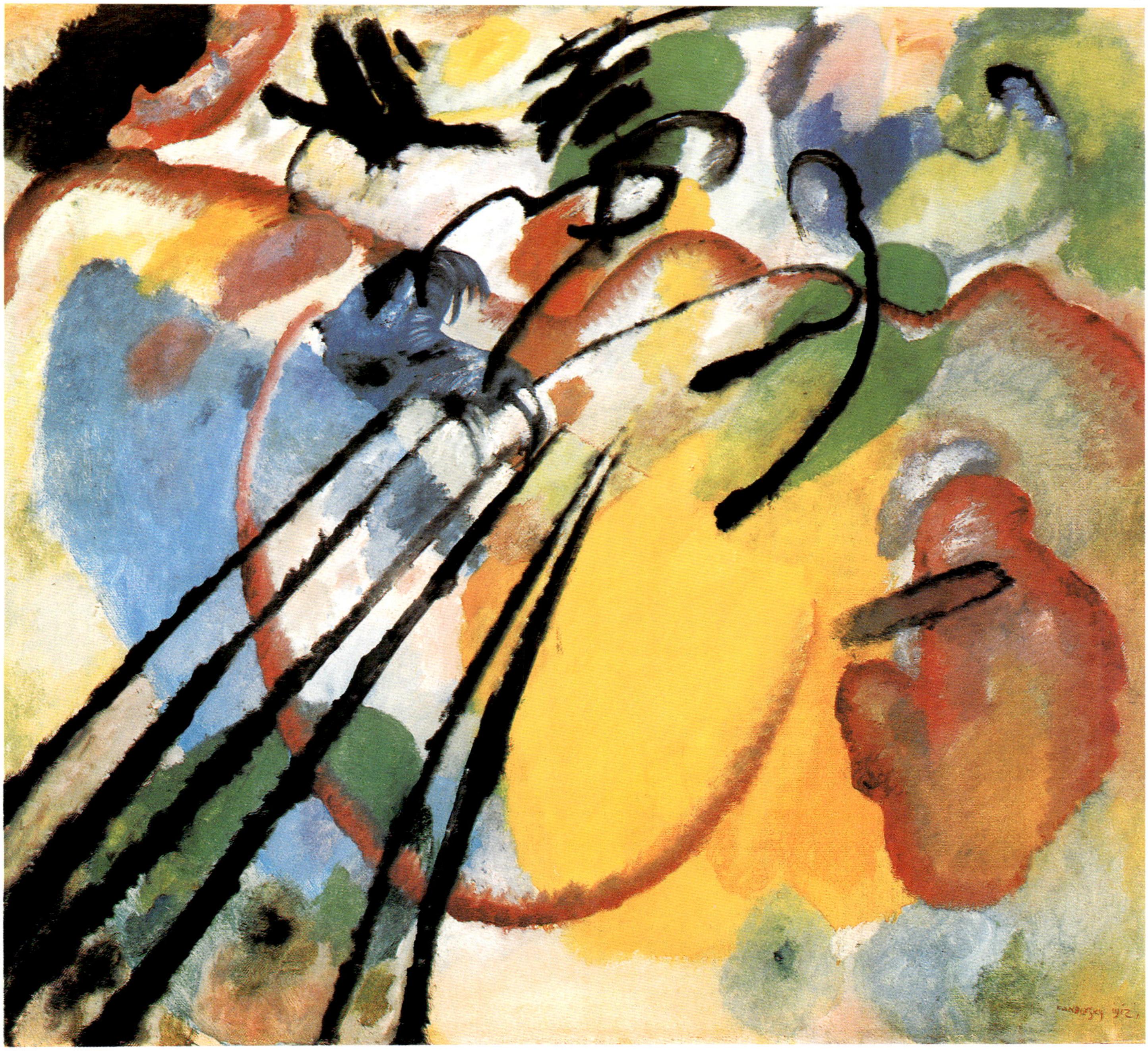

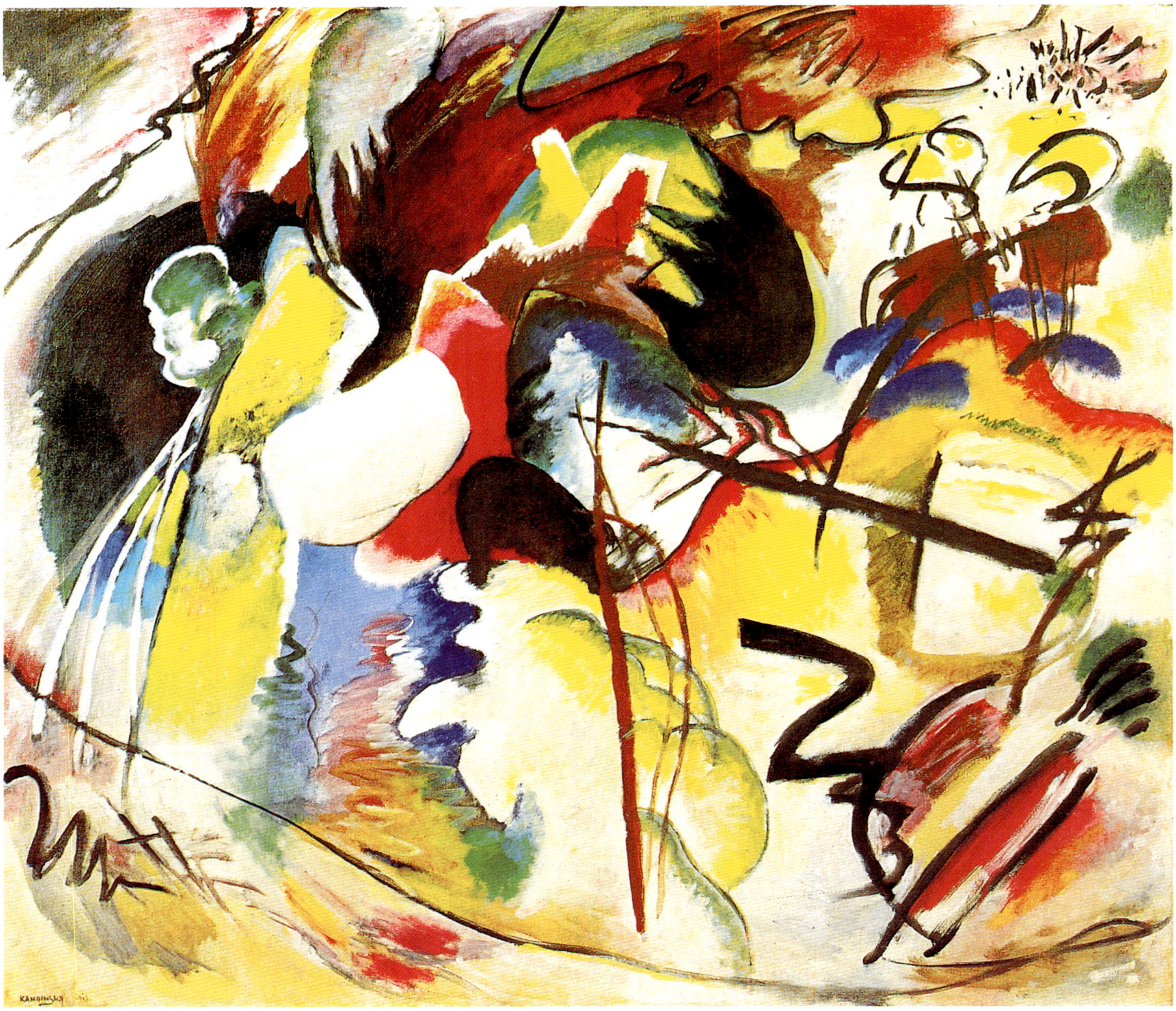

40

41

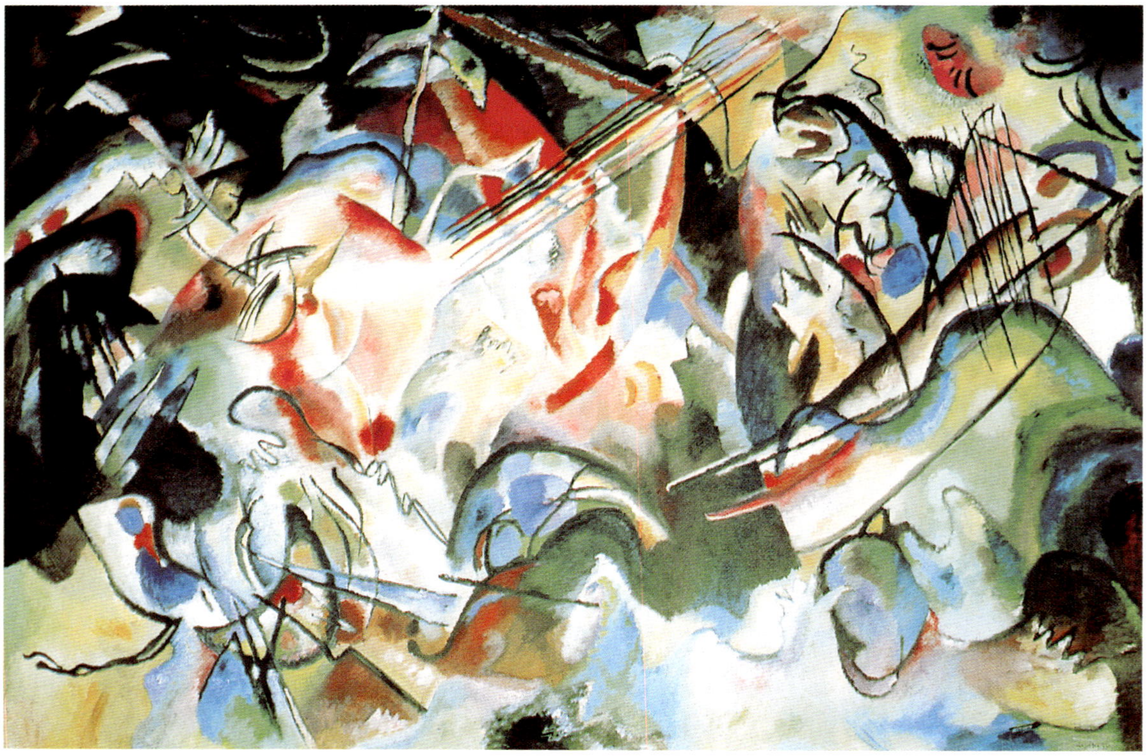

40 Painting with White Form, *1913. The idea of a pictorial core, a vortex upon which all the energies of the painting converge, was one of the earliest organizing principles to appear in Kandinsky's work. Here, the core is the white blot to the left of center.*

41 Composition VI, *1913. Kandinsky called his most complex paintings Compositions, and each was generally preceded by a number of preliminary studies. Works such as this are among his most intricate pictorial structures and can scarcely be appreciated in reproduction.*

42 Fantastic Improvisation, *1913. The dark blot at the center of the painting draws the swirling strokes of color into one central vortex of movement. The more isolated areas in the corners act as a frame for this dominant motion.*

42

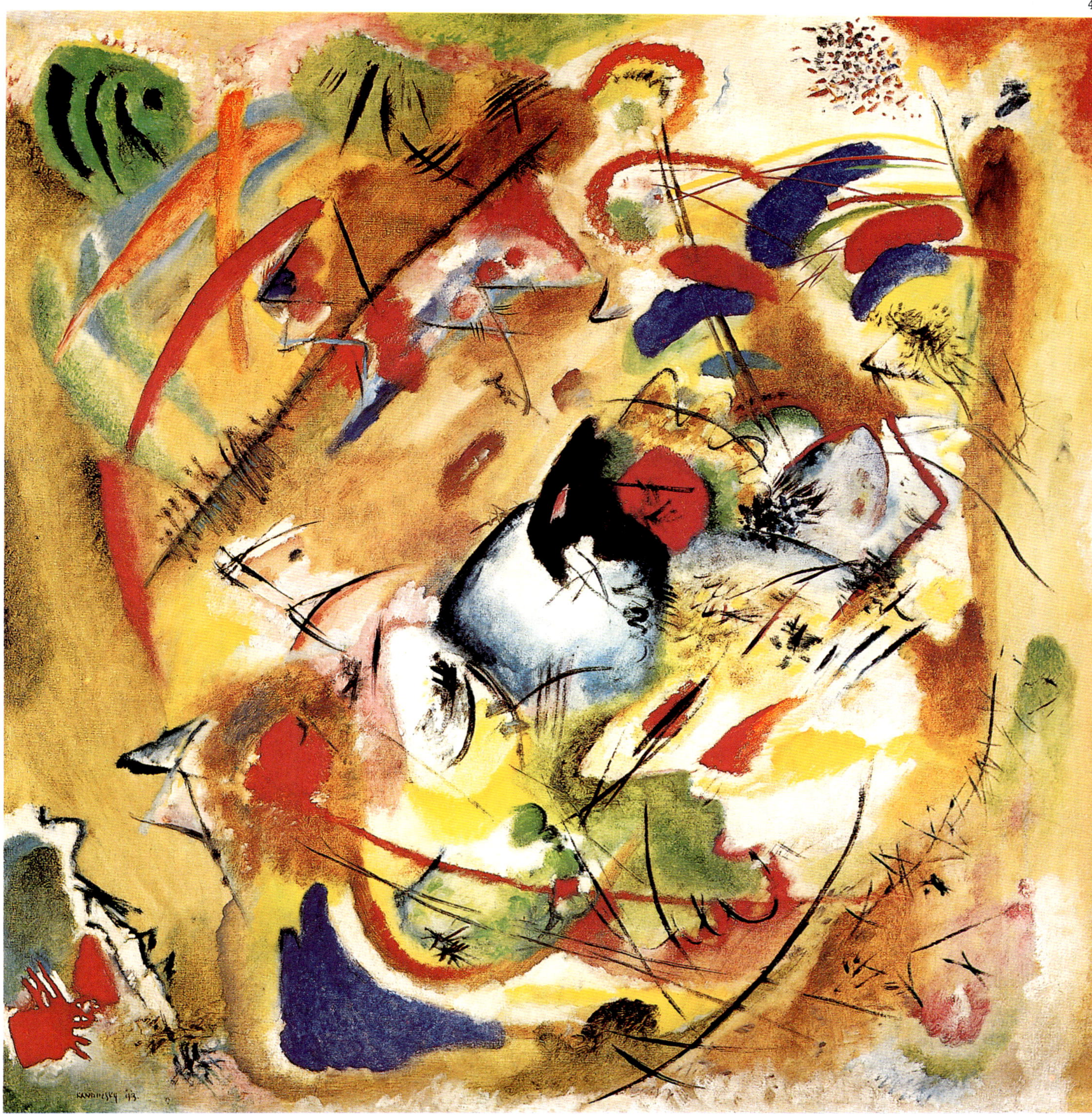

43

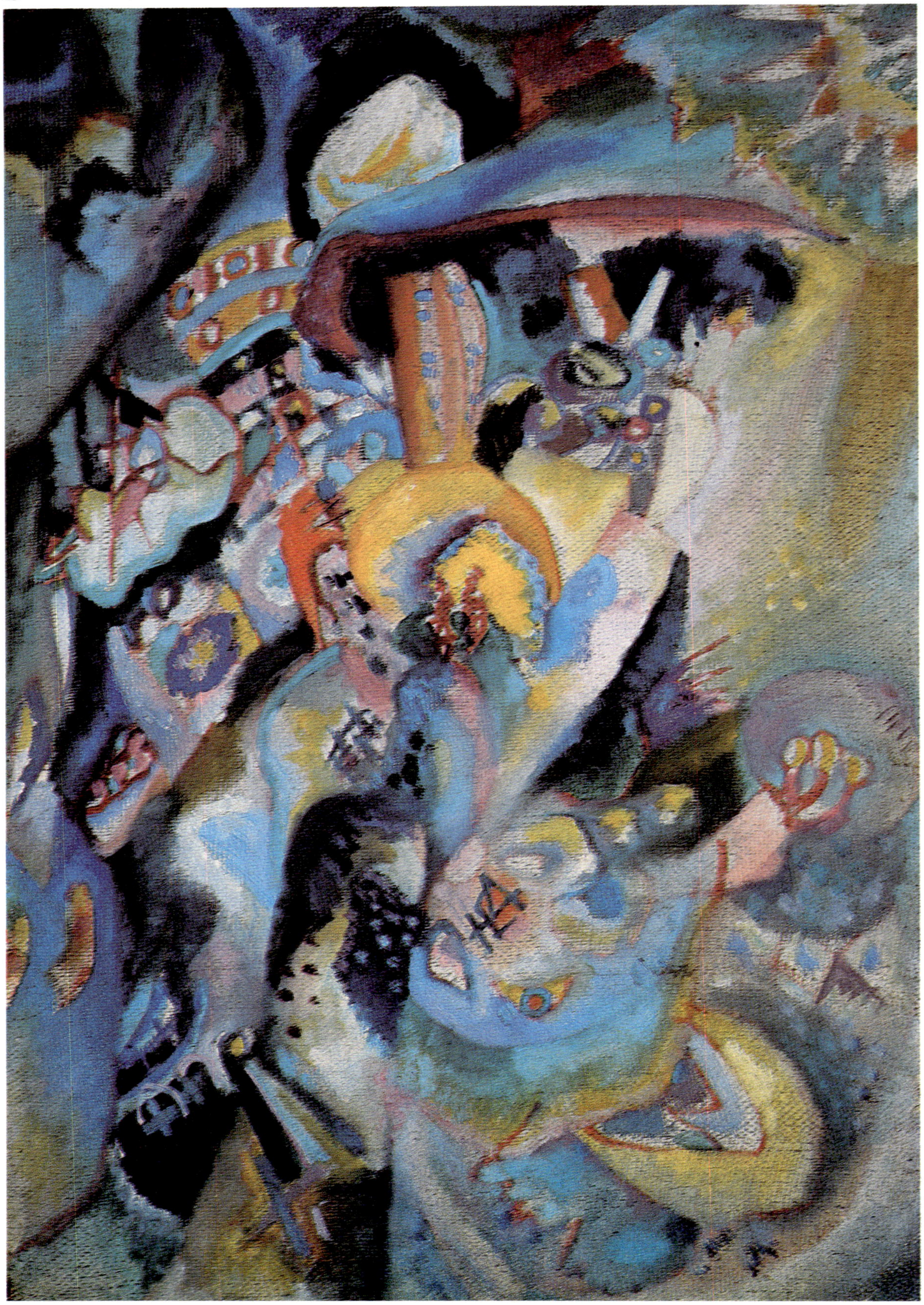

43 Moscow II, *1916. This painting was executed after Kandinsky's return to Russia at the outbreak of World War I. It is illuminating to compare it with his written description of sunset in his native city: "The sun dissolves the whole of Moscow into a single spot, which ... sets all of one's soul vibrating.... It is the last chord of the symphony, which brings every color vividly to life, which allows, even forces, all of Moscow to resound like the final fortissimo of a gigantic orchestra.... To paint this hour, I thought, must be for an artist the most impossible, the greatest joy."*

44 Black Lines I, *1913. The expansiveness that Kandinsky attributed to the color yellow is here offset by the compact density of the reds and blues, which, with their greater compositional "weight," slip toward the bottom. The graphic lines in the work do not conflict with this underlying painted structure, but instead complement it, giving the viewer a schematic means of reading the picture. With each painting, Kandinsky tested anew the relationship between color and line.*

44

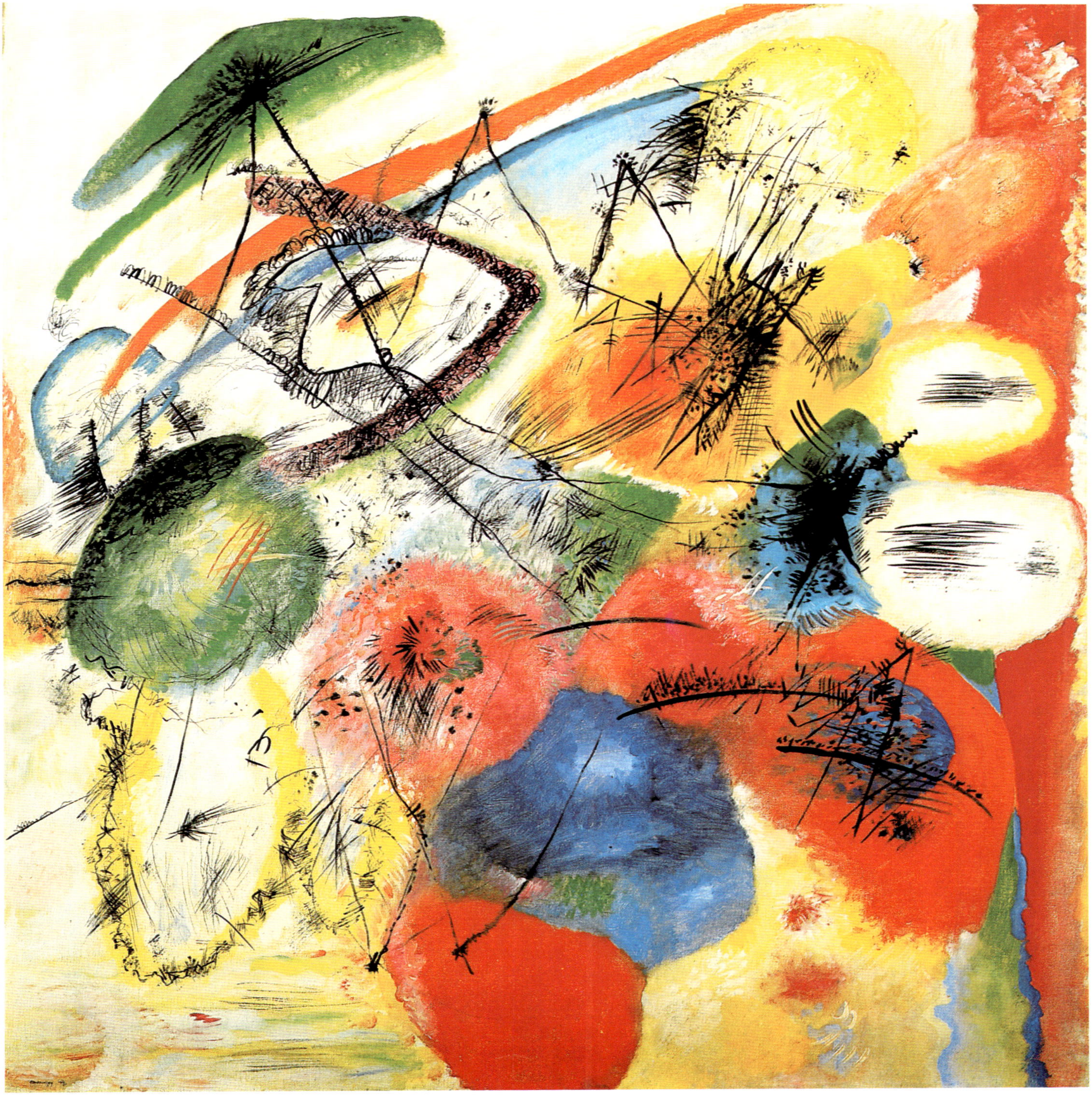

The Folkloric Imagination

During the greater part of his childhood in Russia, Kandinsky was raised by his aunt, Elisabeth Ticheeva, who used to read him Russian and German folktales. In 1889, the Society of Natural Sciences, Ethnography, and Anthropology invited him on a scientific mission to Vologda, in northern Russia, to study agrarian law as well as the surviving traces of pre-Christian religions in the area. These circumstances attest to Kandinsky's early interest in folklore and indigenous culture, among the constants in the Romantic tradition of Northern Europe. In Munich, Kandinsky continued to follow this particular predilection and, as a result, several paintings from his early years depict Russian and German legends and popular figures. It is worth noting his profound interest in the specifically Bavarian tradition, dating from the eighteenth and nineteenth centuries, of depicting naïve, vignette-like religious scenes in the medium of small votive paintings on glass. The almanac published by the Blue Rider in 1912 reproduced works of this kind from the Krötz collection, as well as a series of popular prints of various cultural origins. What Kandinsky looked for in these sources were signs of a spirituality still uncontaminated by subsequent cultural developments. Kandinsky himself, who never forgot the icons of his native Russia, made paintings on glass as well as woodcuts in the old German tradition.

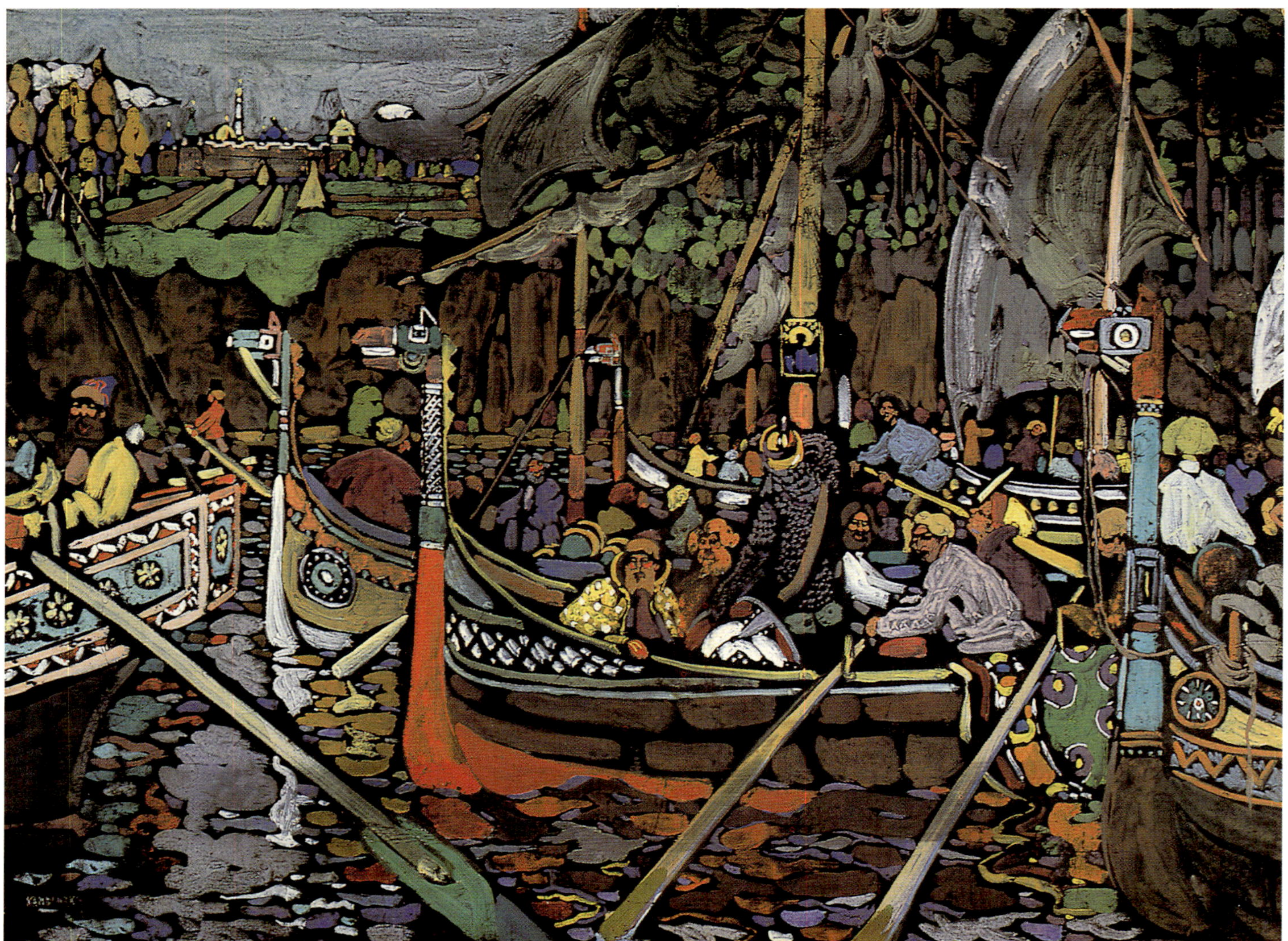

45

45 Song of the Volga, *1906. The painter evokes the atmosphere of the Russian folktales of his childhood and the decorative sensibility typical of the German Jugendstil. Although he lingers over such ornamental features as the icons on the masts or the boats' carved figureheads, the whole scene is nonetheless rendered in a vigorous manner.*

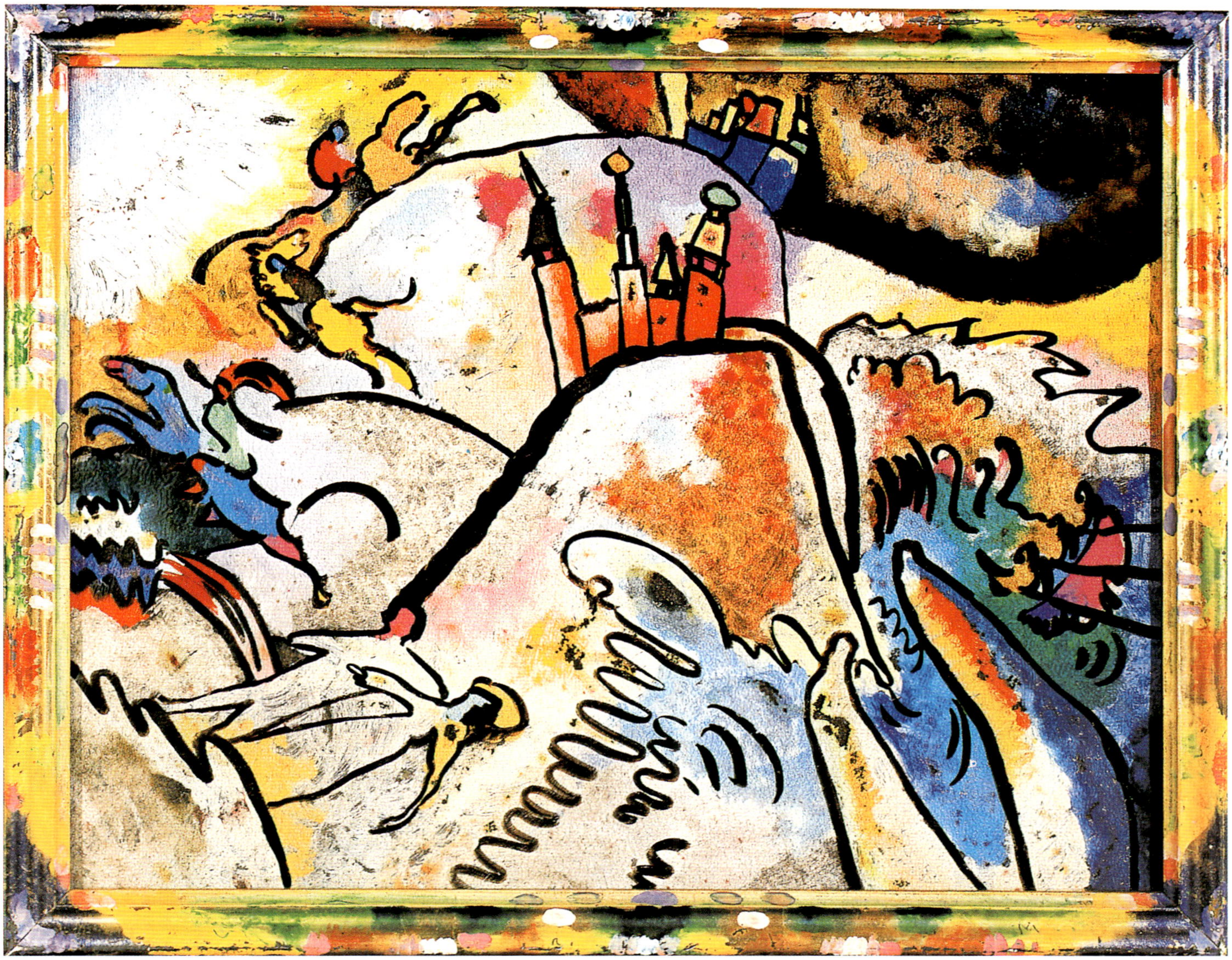

46

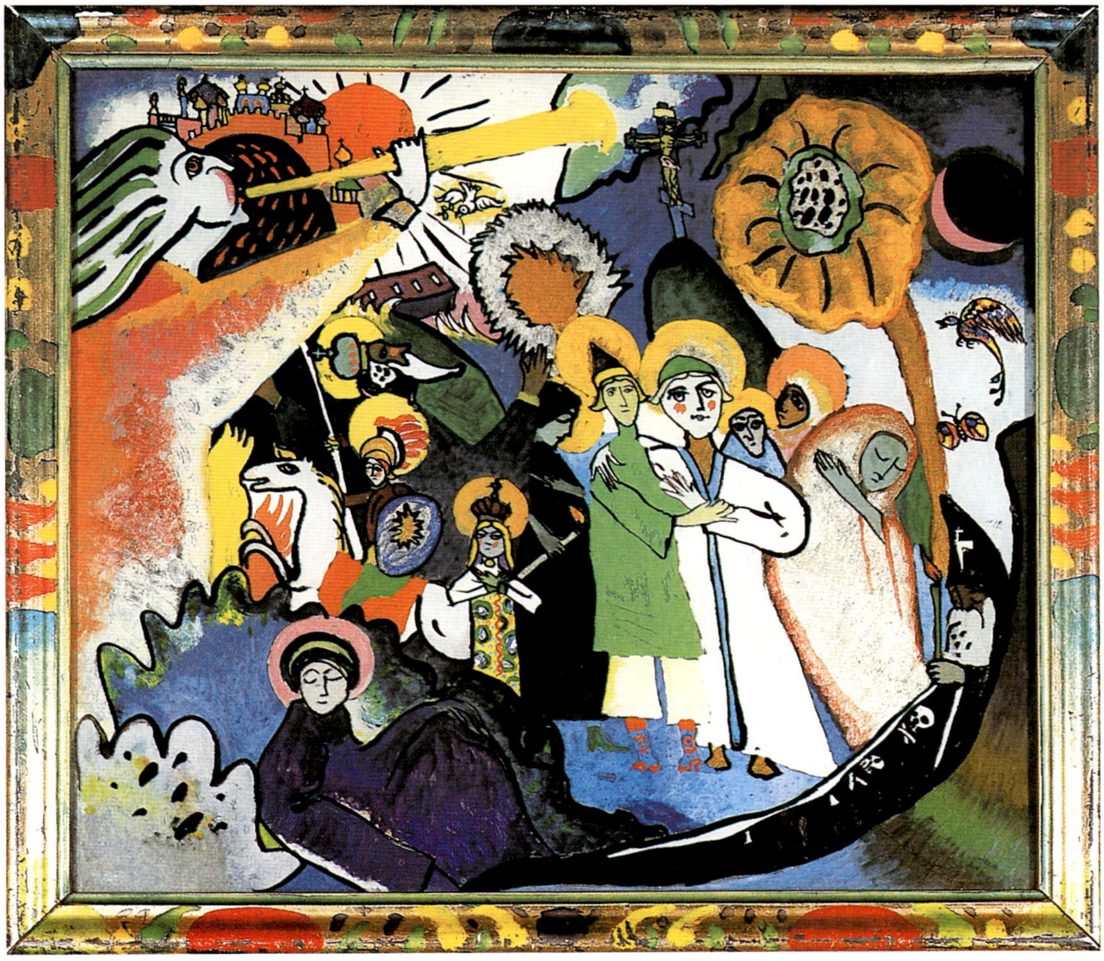

47

46 Glass Painting with Sun, *1910. Bavarian paintings on glass may have put Kandinsky in mind of Russian icons. The idea of painting the frame, however, belongs to a modern tradition according to which a work of art should be a decorative synthesis.*

47 All Saints' Day, *1911. This is Kandinsky's quite straightforward response to the naïve religiosity of the Bavarian paintings on glass from the Krötz collection. However, the same year the artist also painted an abstract version of this scene (plate 29).*

48 Woman in Moscow, *1912. Only rarely did Kandinsky return to figurative art, and when he did it was almost always to deal with memories of his childhood in Russia. The frontal rendition of the central figure here may have been suggested by Russian icons, while the general atmosphere, with mysterious characters floating in midair, is not unlike the fables painted by his countryman Marc Chagall. The choice of colors is quite typical of Kandinsky's other work in those years.*

48

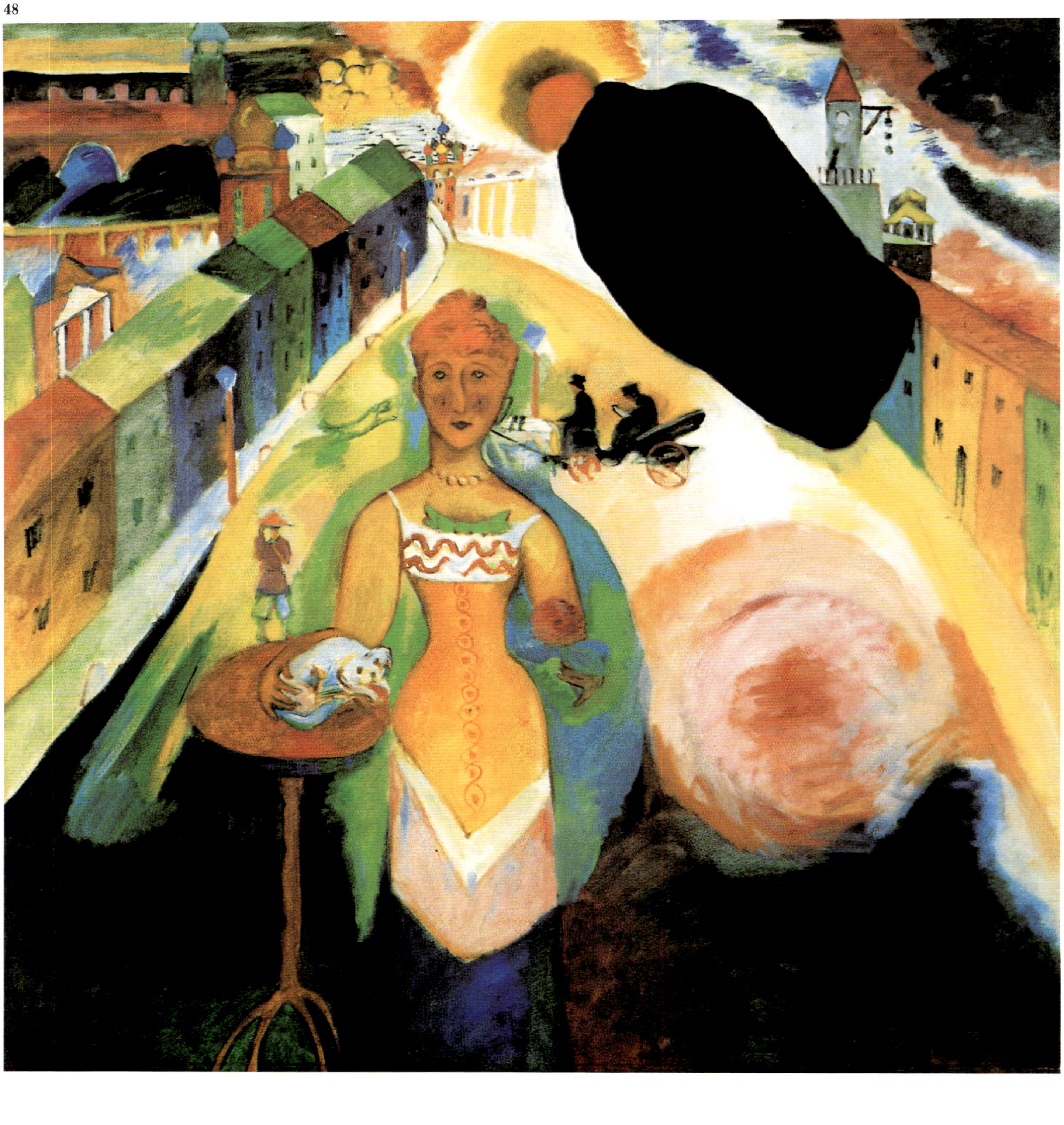

49

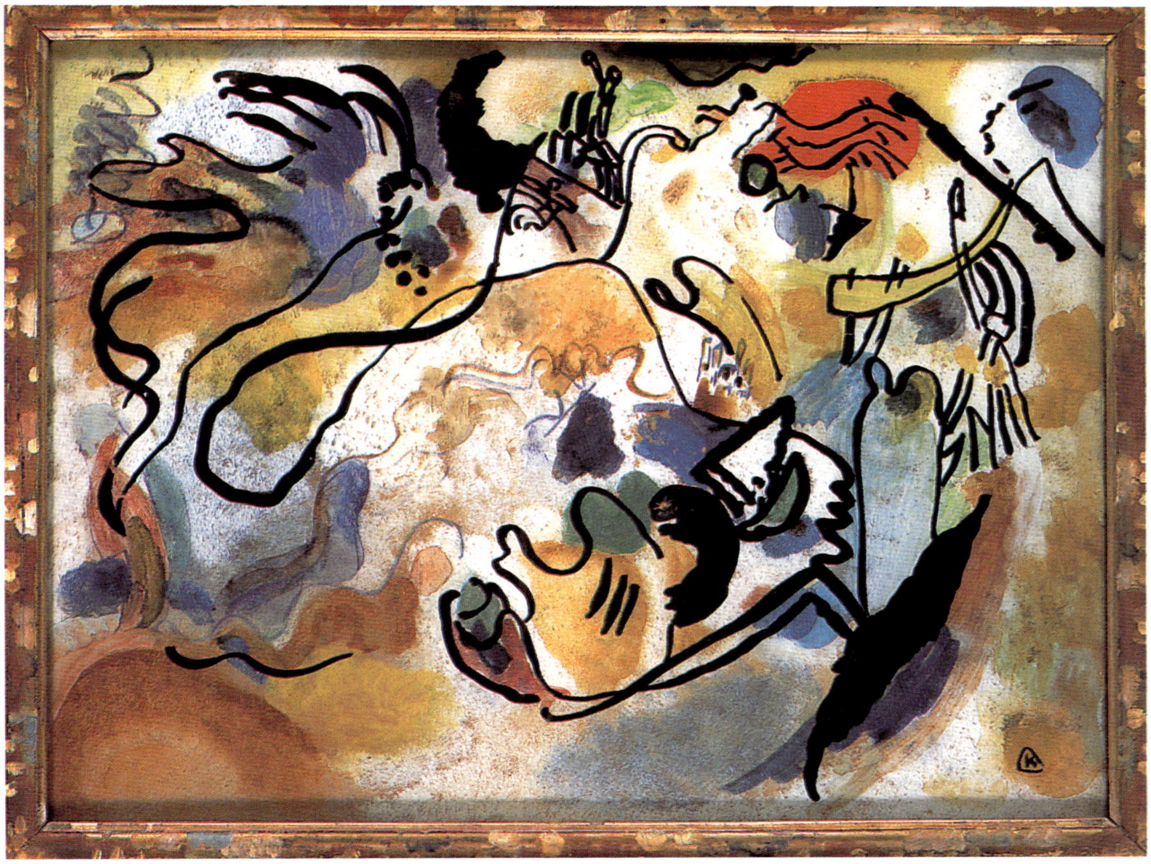

49 Last Judgment, *1912. Apocalyptic imagery recurs frequently in this period of transition toward an abstract art. In this work, both the medium of painting on glass and the decorative treatment of the frame suggest ties to folk culture.*

50 Women in Crinoline, *1918. Painted during his Russian sojourn, this small work on glass is so exceptional as to be accountable only as a form of private diversion. Both the theme and the technique are quite remote from the artist's central preoccupations at the time.*

50

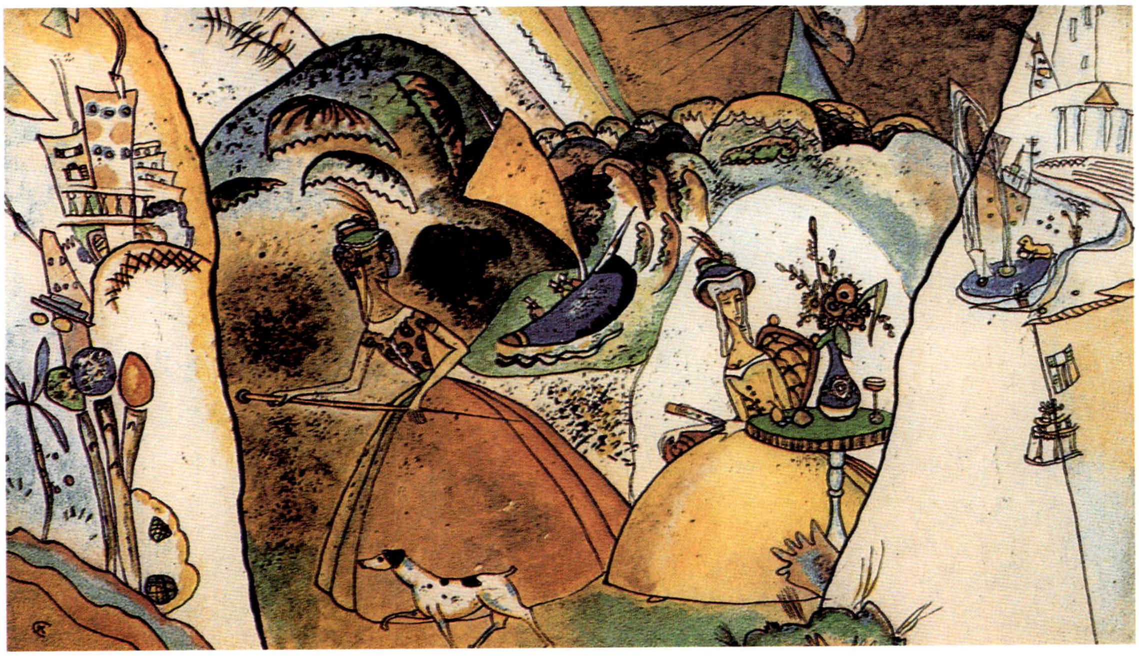

A More Rigorous Style

The years that Kandinsky spent in Russia before again going to Germany, to join the Bauhaus in 1921, were not very productive in terms of the number of works he made. He was kept busy by his responsibilities in the cultural and artistic administration of the new state that had issued from the Revolution. Nonetheless, the paintings that he produced in this period display some significant developments. In spite of his differences with the leading factions of the Russian avant-garde, the influence of their work is clearly felt in the process of systematic analysis that now overtook the flowing chromaticism of the Blue Rider period. Kandinsky wanted to subdue and discipline his masses of color by means of more clearly defined forms. Now, a particular element—an oval or a circle—often became the focus of the composition, and he frequently used the four-sided figure of the trapezoid, and other geometric shapes laid diagonally over the composition, to animate the pictorial surface and define the subject of the painting.

51 In the Gray, *1919. In works like this, previously chaotic compositions begin to become more organized: the placement of the two red areas and the central black one announces the artist's preference for arranging forms along a diagonal. Yet the black strokes and threadlike lines are still reminiscent of Kandinsky's artistic idiom from the Munich period.*

52 White Line, *1920. There is a dynamic tension between the rectangular shape of the canvas itself and the large trapezoid shape that seems to be in front of it and whose corners extend beyond the edges of the painting. This two-layer effect, together with the projecting white arc in the middle, makes the pictorial space seem to bulge outward at the center, as in a relief—a sharp difference from the works of 1910 to 1914.*

51

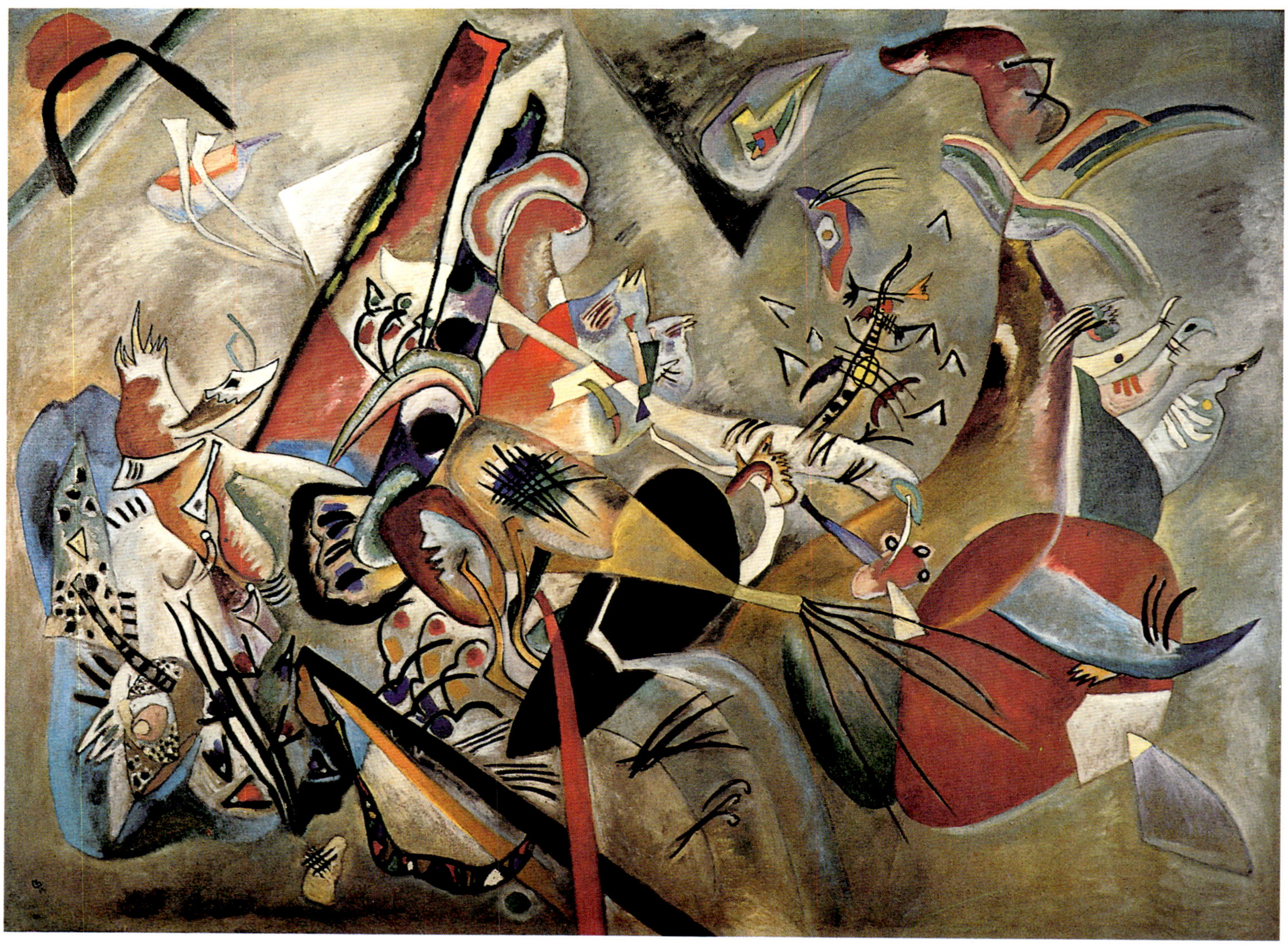

52

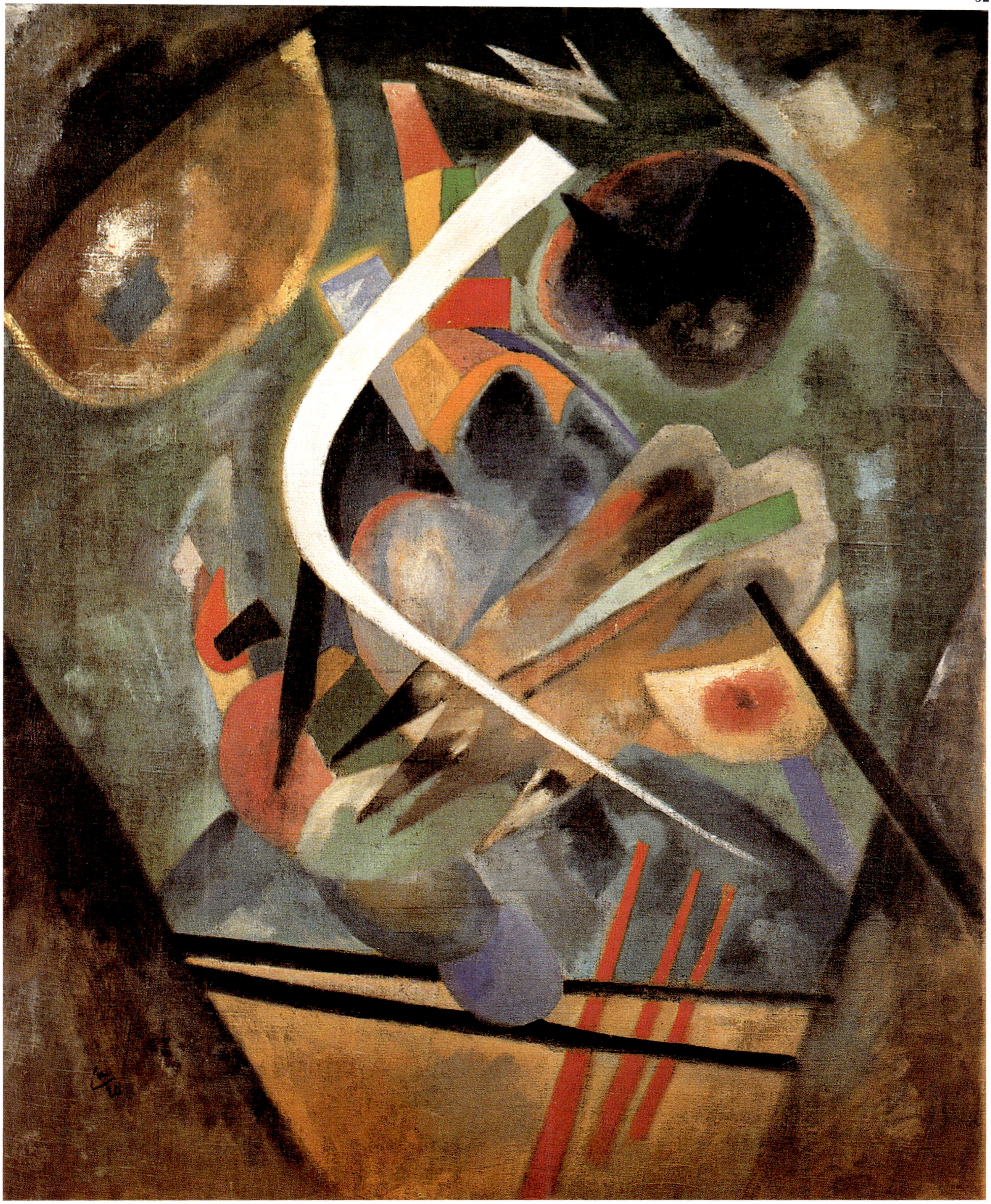

53 Red Oval, *1920. The red oval is a variation on the vortex element familiar from Kandinsky's earlier paintings, but the large yellow plane that organizes the picture as a whole heralds a new, increasingly geometric style. Though the elements of Kandinsky's vocabulary had changed little since the Munich period, he was composing with them in a new way.*

54 Maquette of a Mural for the Unjuried Exhibition, *1922. Shortly after returning to Germany, Kandinsky executed a mural painting for the reception hall of the unjuried "Berlin Free Exhibition," one of his few works designed as a decoration. The same year, he took charge of the Decorative Painting Workshop at the Bauhaus.*

55 Black Pattern, *1922. A trapezium divided into tiny cells—to be filled in with colors in later paintings—here becomes the center toward which the other shapes gravitate. The geometrically conceived forms are arranged on overlapping planes. The seeming evocation of ships and fish in the lower left corner is a touch of capricious irony rather than a genuine figurative reference.*

53

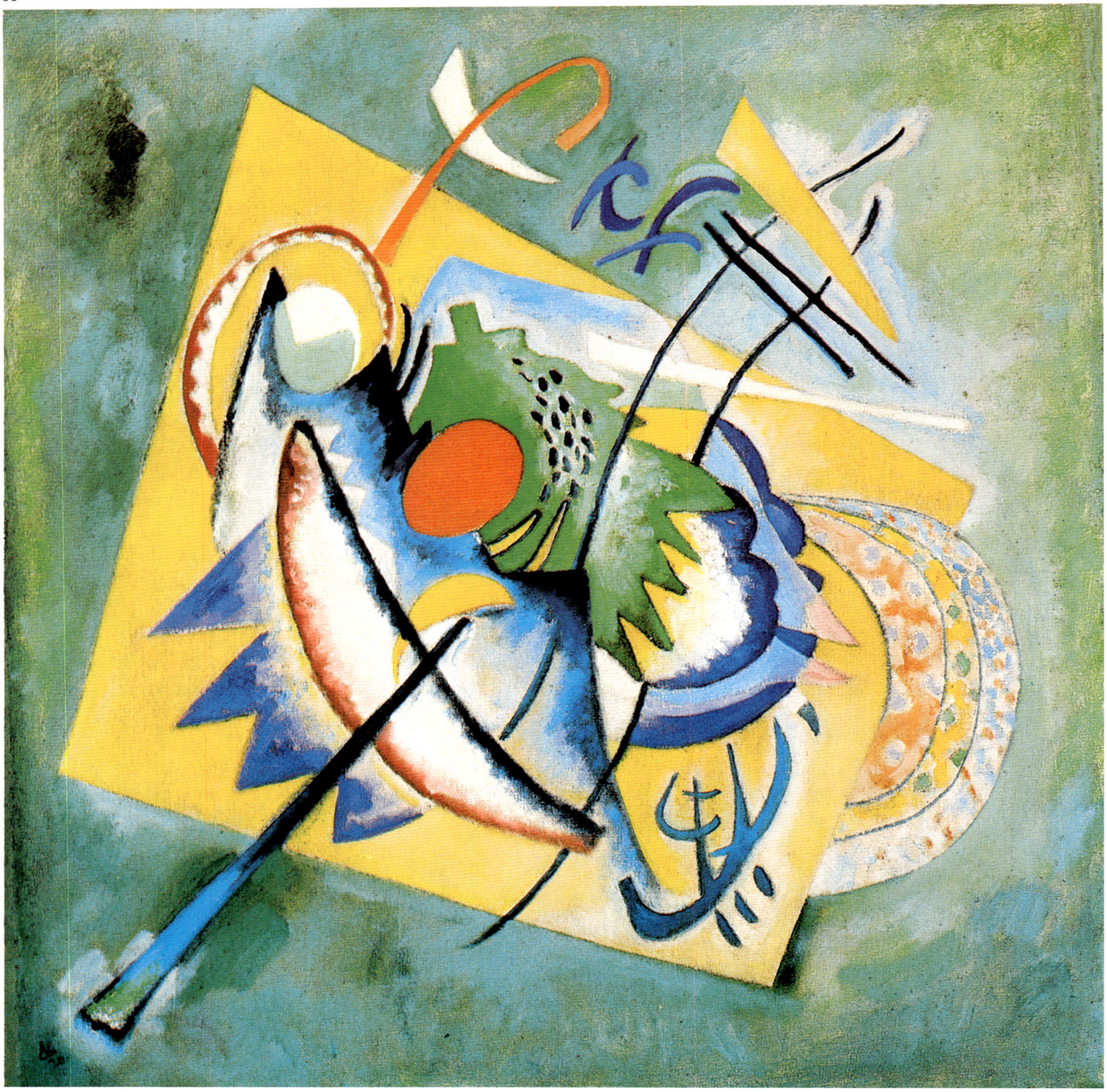

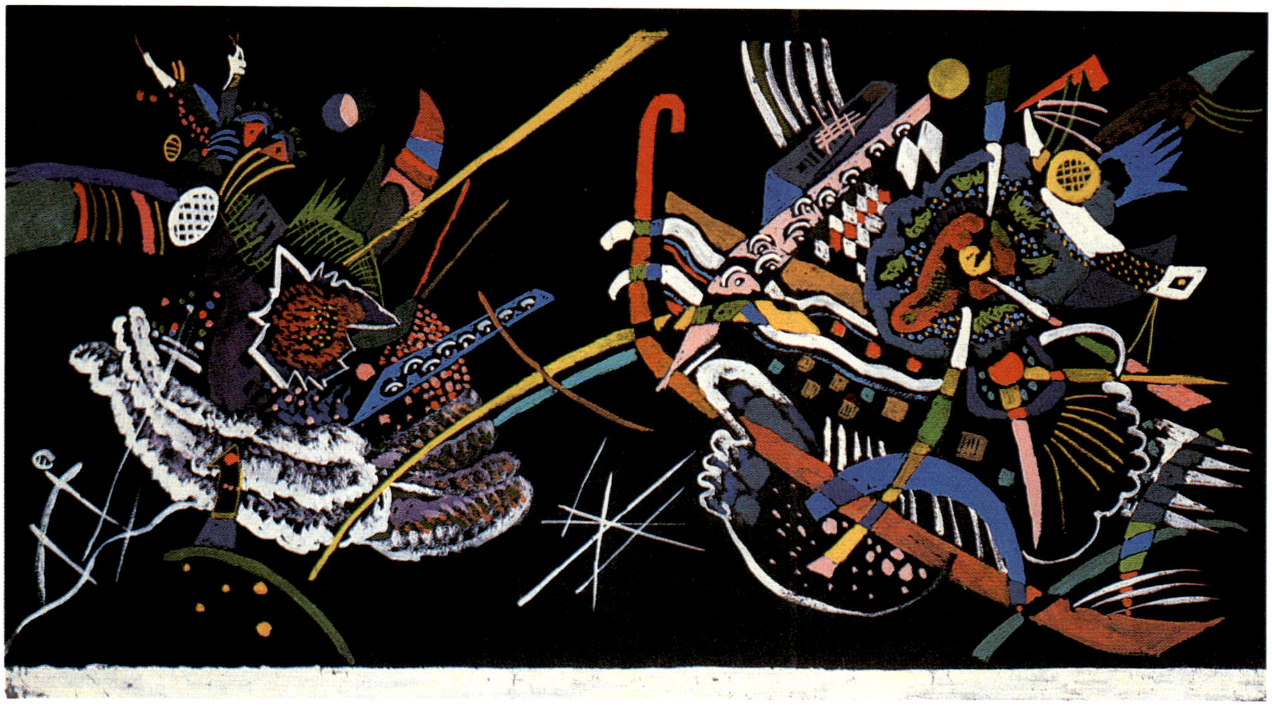

54

55

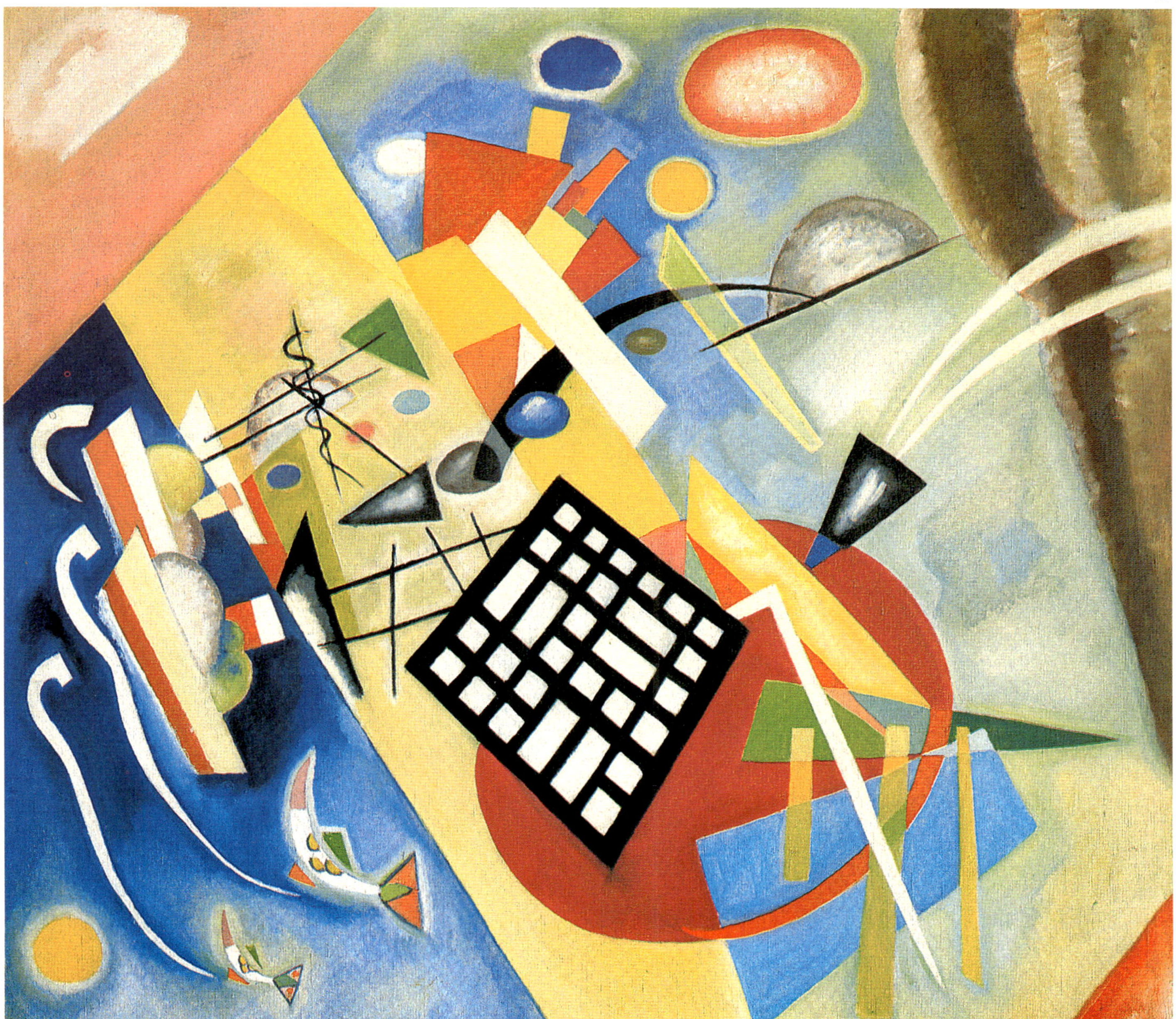

Point and Line to Plane

Kandinsky worked for eleven years—from 1922 to 1933—at the Bauhaus, first in Weimar and then in Dessau and Berlin. His experiences led him to systematize his practices as a painter into a body of teaching, most notably in the book *Point and Line to Plane*, published in 1926. The notion of musical and emotional equivalents to color, initially expounded in *On the Spiritual in Art*, continued to be at the core of his painting, but now this idea was combined with a new interaction of forms. Kandinsky had long pursued a theory of color based on an opposition between red and blue. With his increasing reliance on geometric shapes, he could use them to either intensify or reduce the inherent properties of each color, as well as mark directions and points of tension on the pictorial surface. He was careful, however, not to rely too heavily on theory, applying it freely, without falling into the trap of making painting the mechanical implementation of a formula.

56 Composition VIII, *1923. In this period of Kandinsky's career, the circle appears as a symbol of perfection, often carrying cosmic connotations. The vibrant color of the Blue Rider years is now applied more evenly and smoothly. The economy and exactitude of the geometric style establish a new sense of the absolute.*

57 On White II, *1923. Two heavy black lines convey the twisting effect created by the brown trapezoid as it tilts away from the picture plane. The turning of the triangles and quadrilaterals in space reflects this tension, and where they overlap there is a complex mingling of their colors. For Kandinsky, the expressive character of his art, its drama, arose from these dynamic interactions between shapes and colors. "The encounter of a circle with the point of a triangle," he wrote, "is no less affecting than God's finger touching Adam's in the work of Michelangelo."*

56

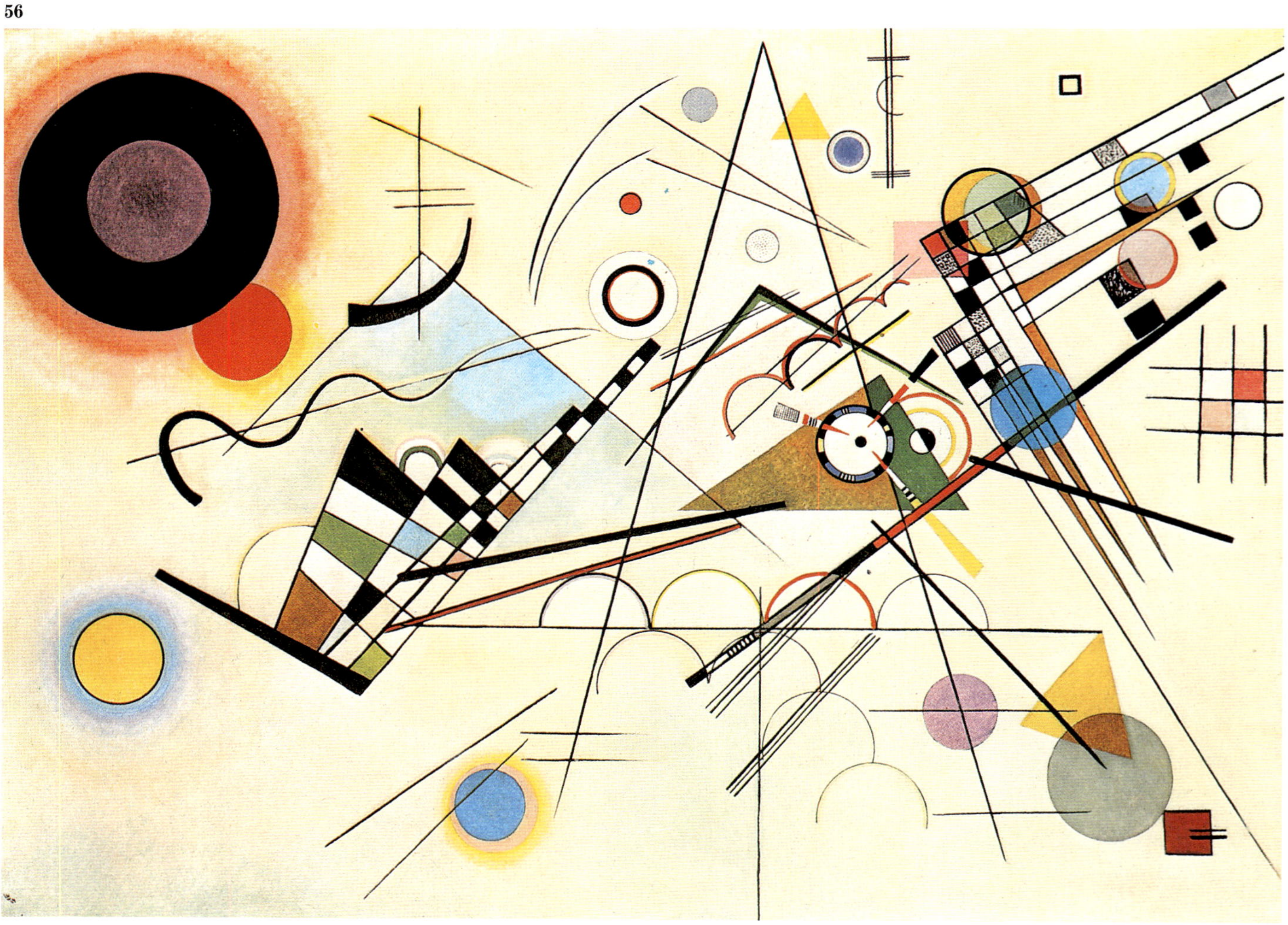

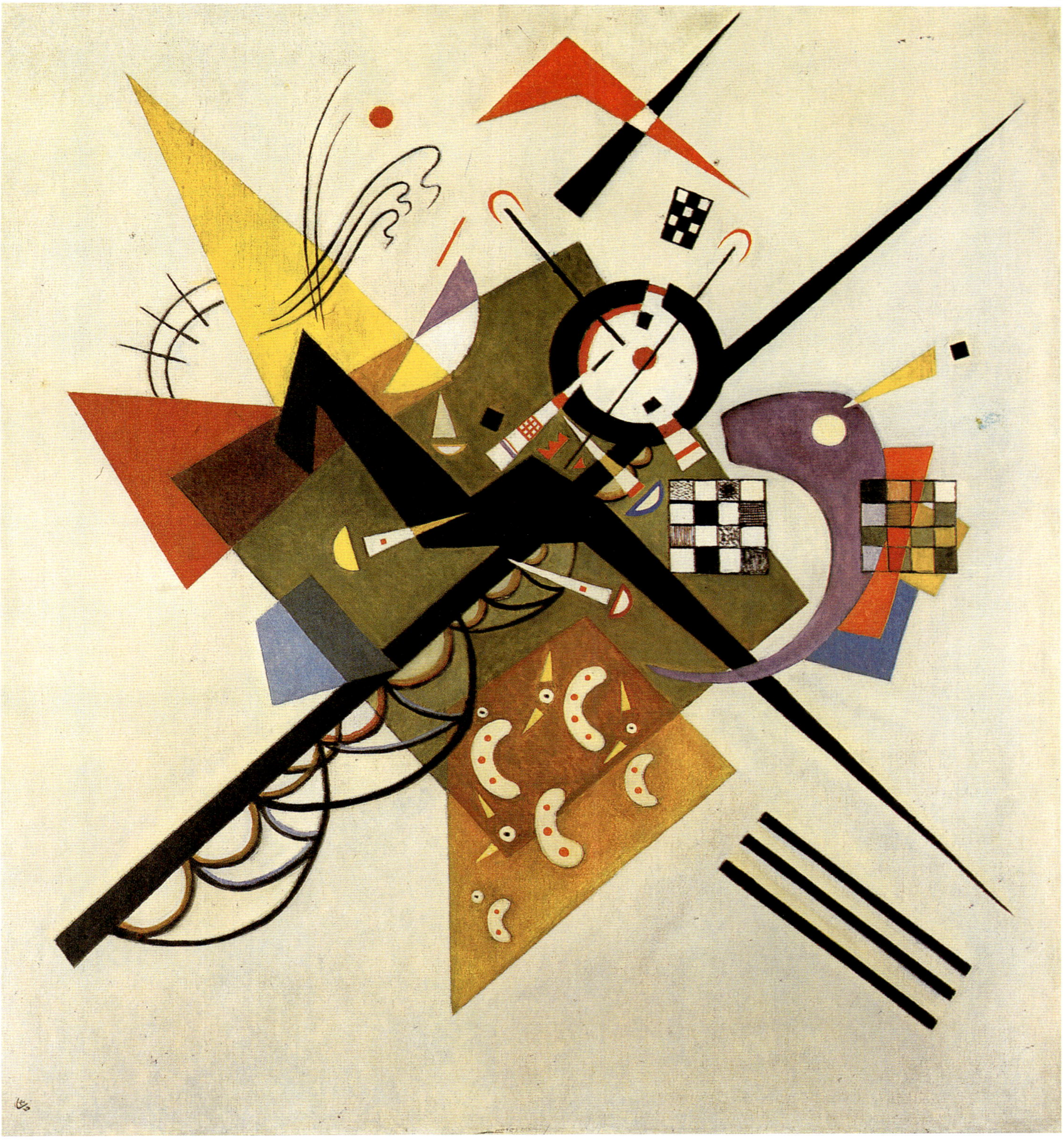

58

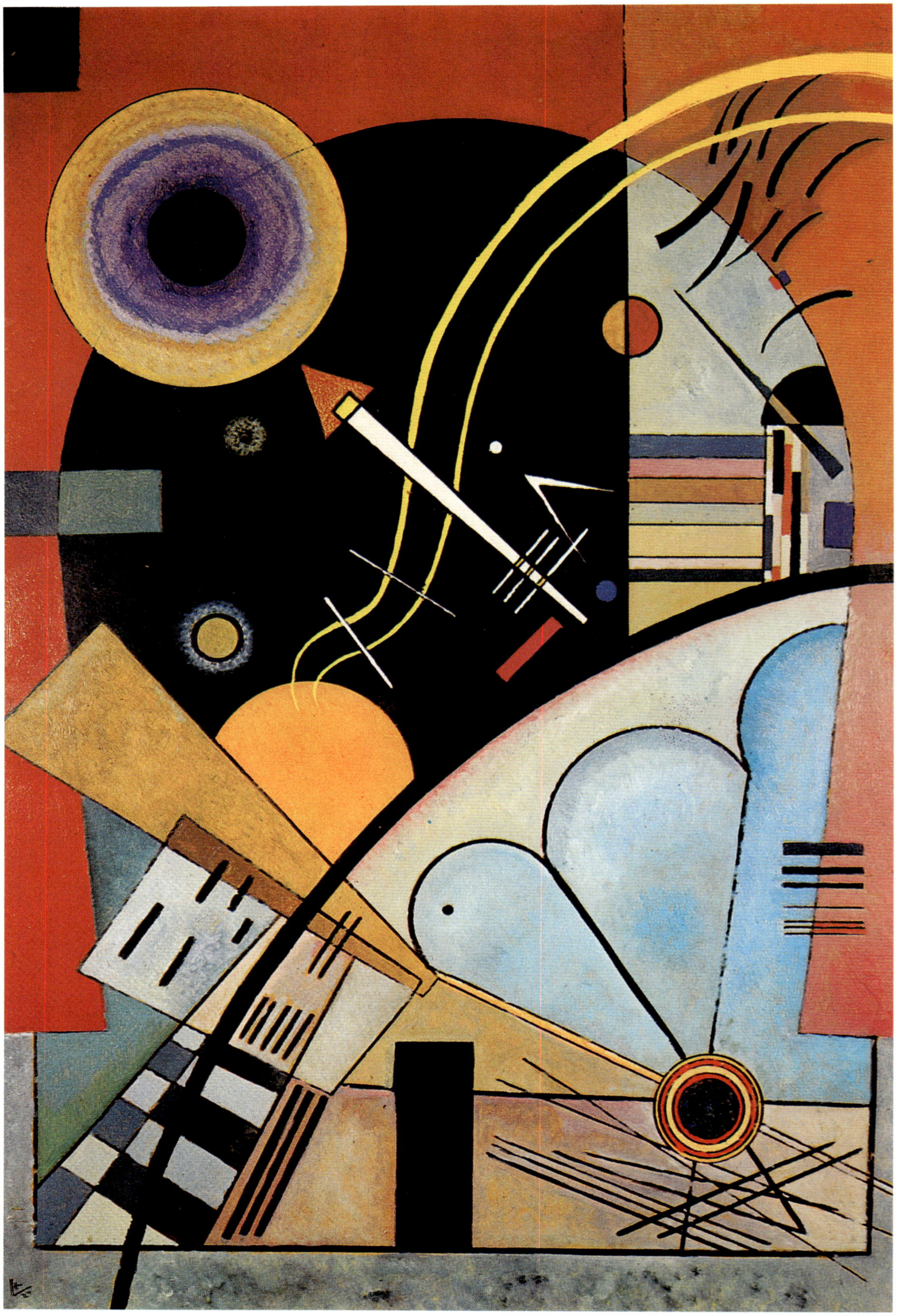

58 Still Tension, *1924. As the title of this painting suggests, its pictorial structure demonstrates the balance between opposing forces. The complex interplay in the picture between superimposed forms—a welter of straight lines set against curves and circles against rectangles—is resolved by the equilibrium between the two principal circles, set in opposite corners. The strong diagonal axis that connects the two is emphasized by an arrow. The colors, too, are arranged in accordance with this opposition, so that the "warmer" reds and yellows predominate in the upper left and the "cooler" blues in the lower right. Within this color scheme, the two circles serve as alternatives: a cold vortex and a hot one. The compositional clarity sought in this type of painting is a result both of Kandinsky's evolution as an artist and his concurrent experience as a teacher.*

59 Hard But Soft, *1927. Once again, the structural precision is reminiscent of the work of the Russian Constructivists. The intricate network of straight lines, circles, and triangles generates a pattern of small, separate cells, many of them filled in with color. The title suggests how the hardness of this geometric structure is played off against the softness of the open, diaphanous background.*

59

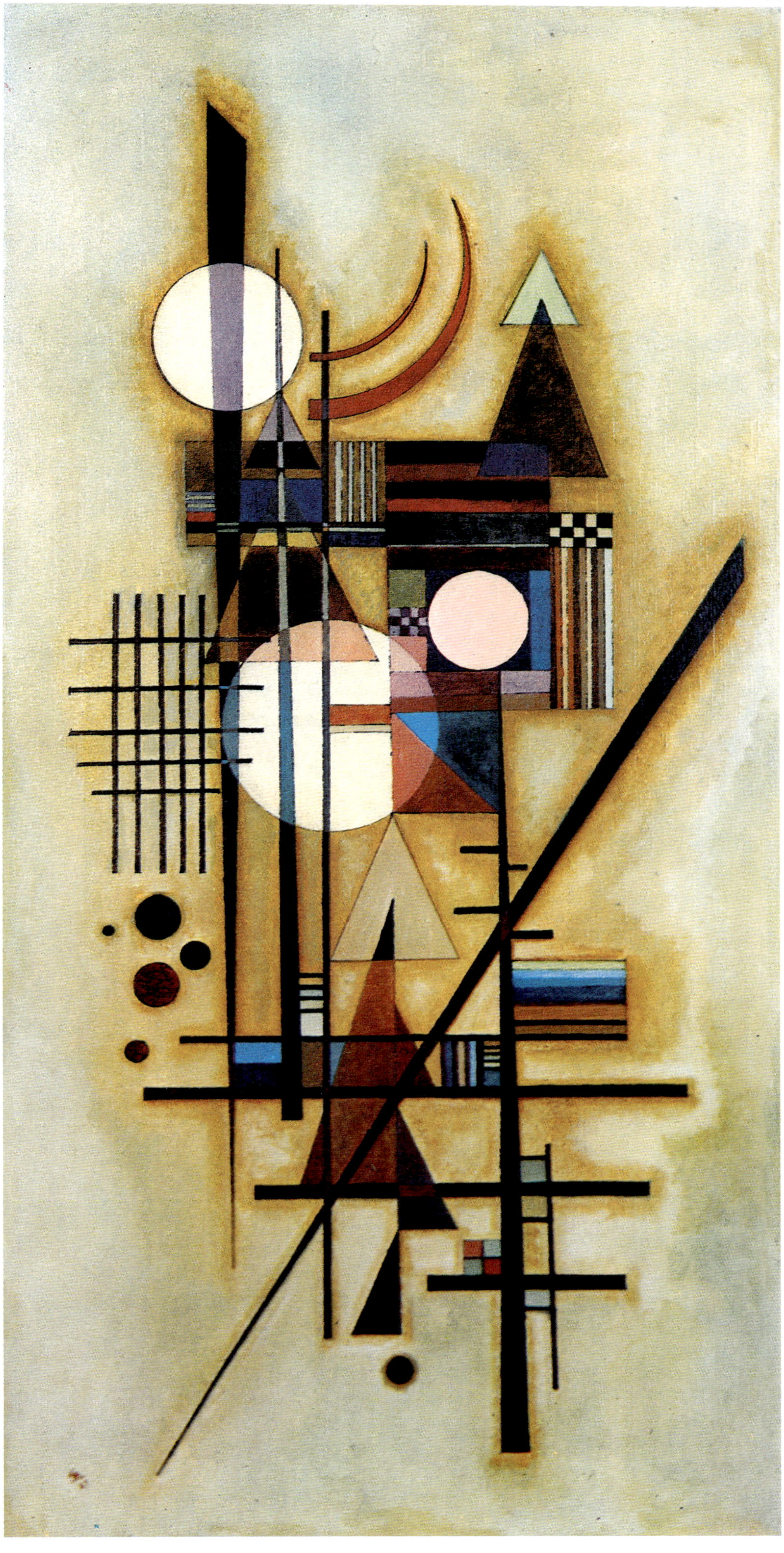

60 Several Circles, *1926. Spheres and disks begin to appear in Kandinsky's work with the 1922 graphic portfolio* Little Worlds *(see page 6), whereby he sought to reconcile the intellectual rigor of the Bauhaus with his own spiritualistic impulses. Thus, in one sense, geometric shapes such as the circle are the products of the rational mind, part of the system of mathematical measurement first developed by the ancient Greeks. Yet at the same time, as Kandinsky said, "a circle ... is a blazing patch of sky"—a solar disk, like the sun, endowed with cosmic overtones and thus a way of picturing, and understanding, the workings of the universe.*

61 Thirteen Rectangles, *1930. As if reversing the course of his development, Kandinsky seems to return to a kind of rigor from which he was actually more distant than he may seem. This work may suggest the Neoplasticist compositions of Piet Mondrian and Theo van Doesburg, but the staircase arrangement of the rectangles, which appears in a number of paintings, also invokes an occult notion of initiation and spiritual progress. As in most works from this period, the entire composition is organized around one element, in this case the large, red square near the center.*

60

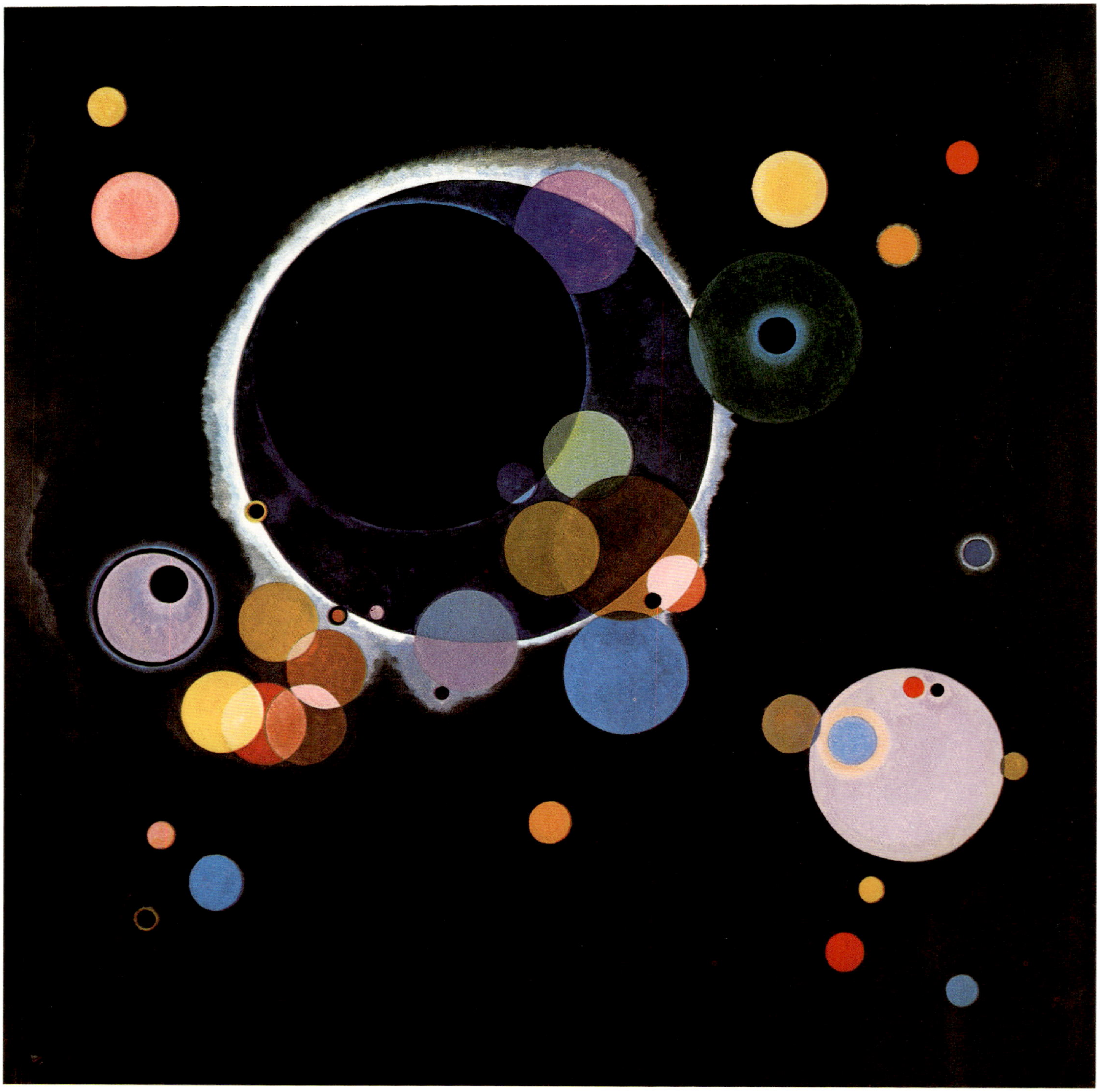

61

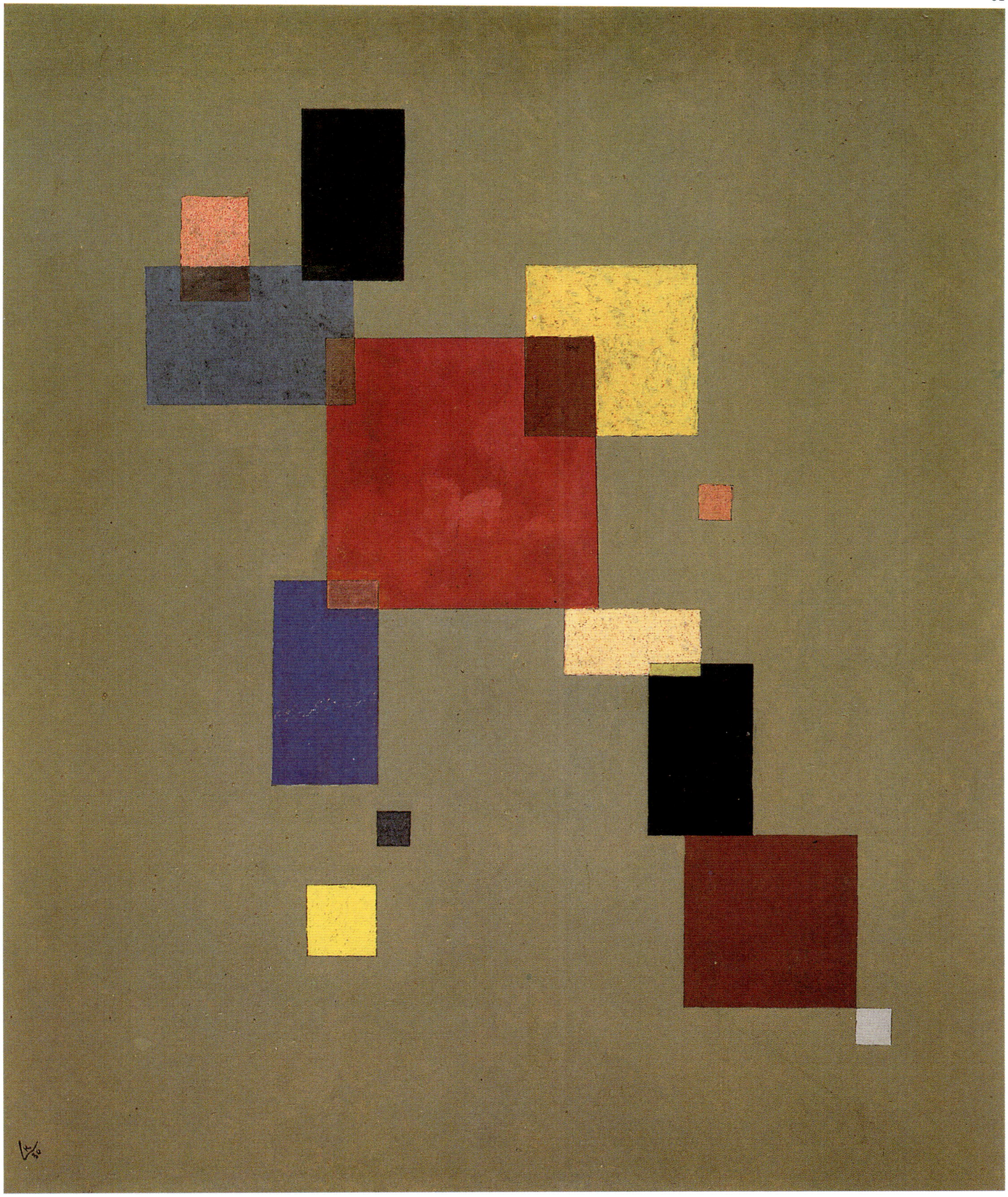

A New Freedom

Kandinsky's relation to European abstract painting after he settled in Paris in 1933 was not an easy one. Although, by that time, he was an established artist, his social circle in the French capital was rather restricted. In spite of that, however, his late works are characterized by the special freedom and tranquility sometimes seen in an artist's old age. Kandinsky abandoned the strict geometry that had distinguished the Bauhaus years and started practicing what can be called a "biomorphic" abstraction, on account of its softly organic, sinuous shapes. For some viewers, these images evoke the world revealed by the microscope, an association which may indeed have attracted the artist as an alternative to immediate perception, a fantastic universe concealed from the unaided senses. What the mysterious yet festive lyricism of these paintings really seeks, however, is the "inner gaze," that transcendental goal that Kandinsky had pursued throughout his career. In 1910, writing about the content of his paintings, he said that he wanted "to speak of secrets by means of a secret. Could this be the theme? Is this not the objective, conscious or unconscious, of the urgent creative impulse? With the language of art one can speak to humanity about what is beyond the human."

62

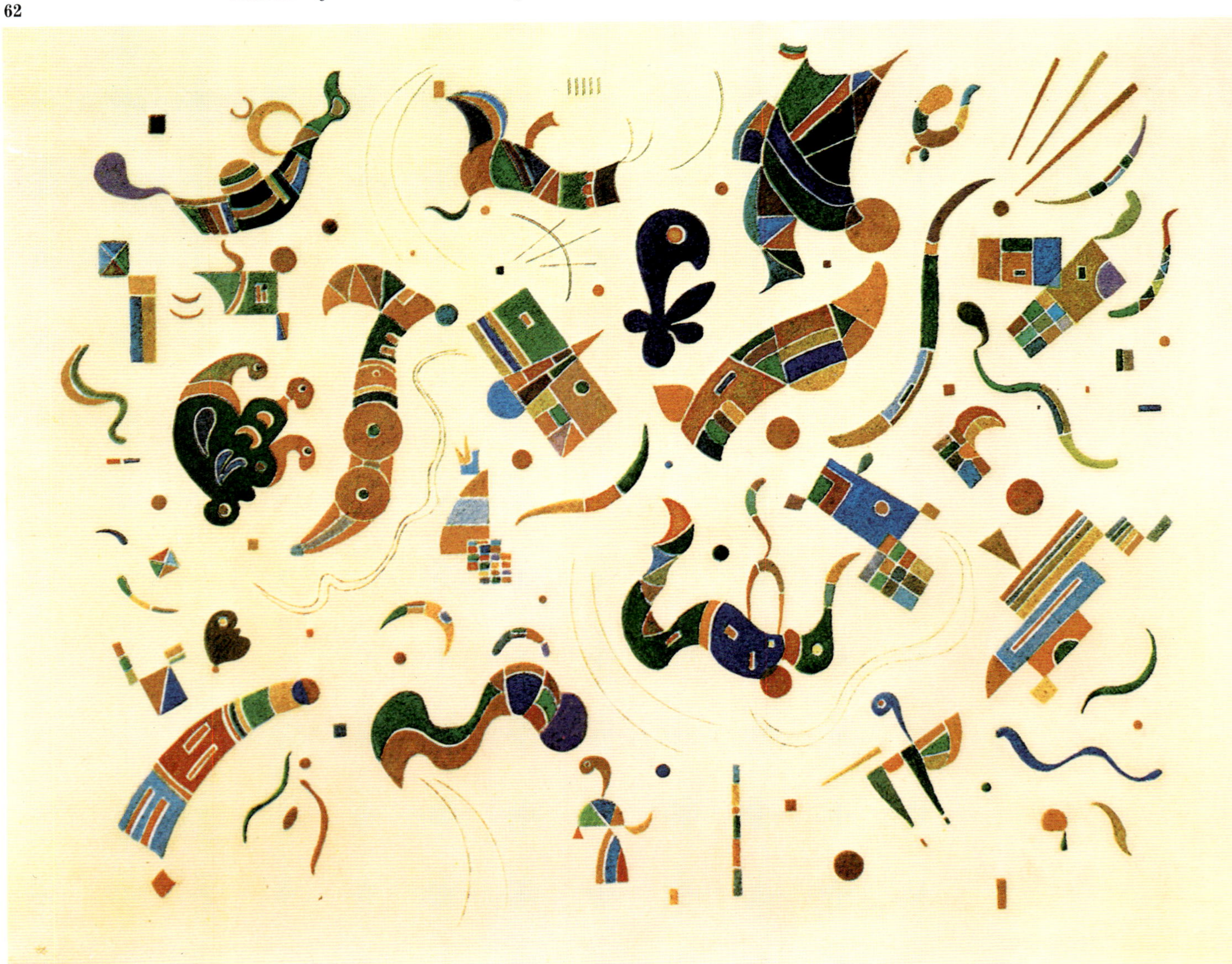

62 Interrelations, *1934. The small, dynamic, and brightly colored organic forms recall the appearance of protozoa, the tiny cells seen through the lens of a microscope. One cannot discount the influence of artists such as Jean Arp and Joan Miró, whom Kandinsky met during his years in Paris, but the principles governing the color relations remain the same as in his own previous works.*

63 Graceful Ascent, *1934. The stepped arrangement of shapes seen in* Thirteen Rectangles *(plate 61) returns here, but now it is presented in a more uninhibited manner, like one of the miniature universes, full of wit, devised by Paul Klee. The suggestion of a spiral, created by the three small crescents above the central square, subtly enhances the sense of upward movement, while also indicating the kind of vortex that Kandinsky had employed in many of his paintings since the Munich years.*

63

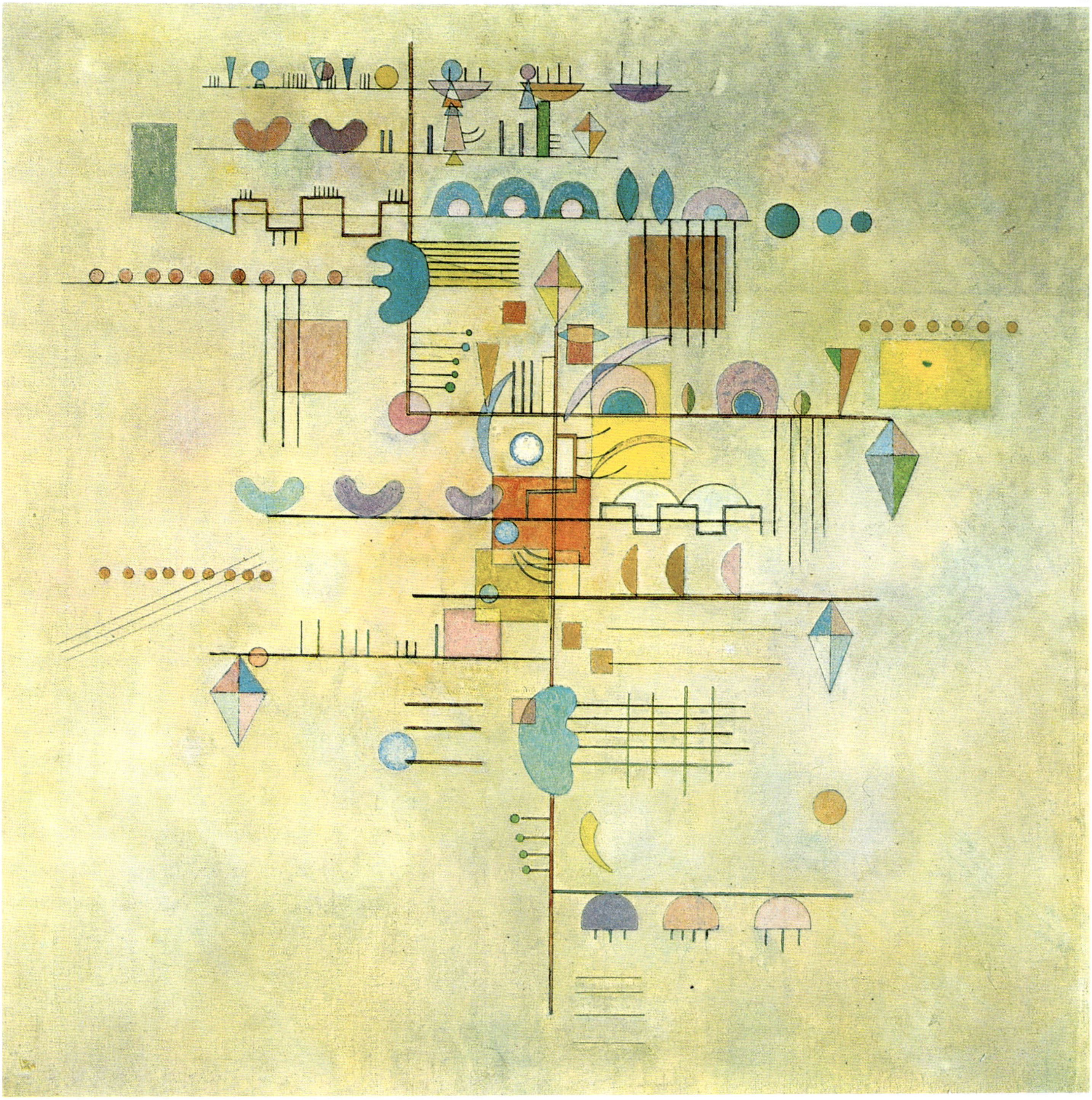

64

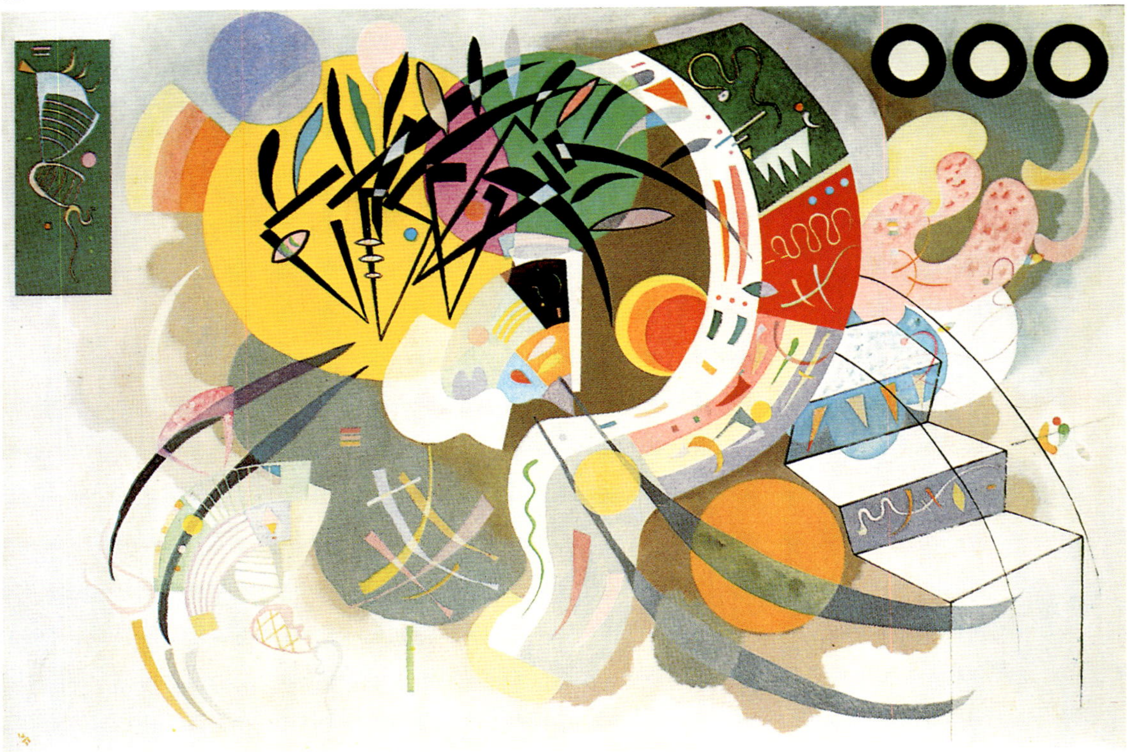

64 Dominant Curve, *1936. The symbolic staircase, most evident at the lower right, here incorporates both geometric and organic forms. Though Kandinsky remained indebted to the compositional rigor of the Bauhaus, he also valued the greater freedom of the new idiom that he had now mastered.*

65 Accompanied Milieu, *1937. The familiar symbolism of the circle gives rise to myriad curvilinear shapes, the dominant one resembling the staff of a musical score, all set against a bright yellow field, like the gold background of an icon.*

65

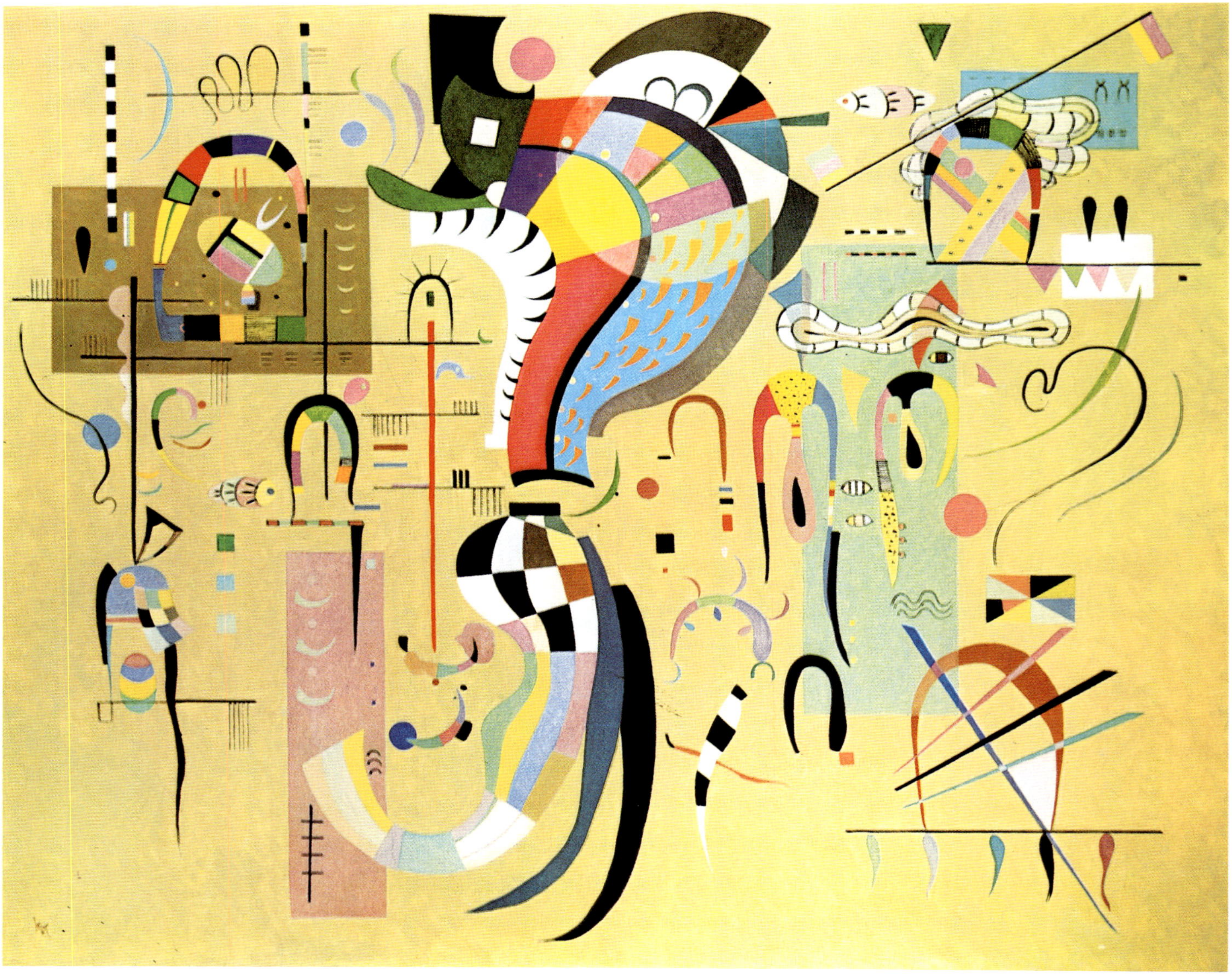

66 The White Line, *1936. Kandinsky here makes use of the distinctively modernist whipping curve, so frequent, for instance, in the decorative works of August Endell, whom Kandinsky met during his first years in Munich. The biomorphic form under the white line, with its related indenting curves, evokes both the contours and the texture of a micro-organism, although recently it has been reinterpreted as a horse and rider.*

66

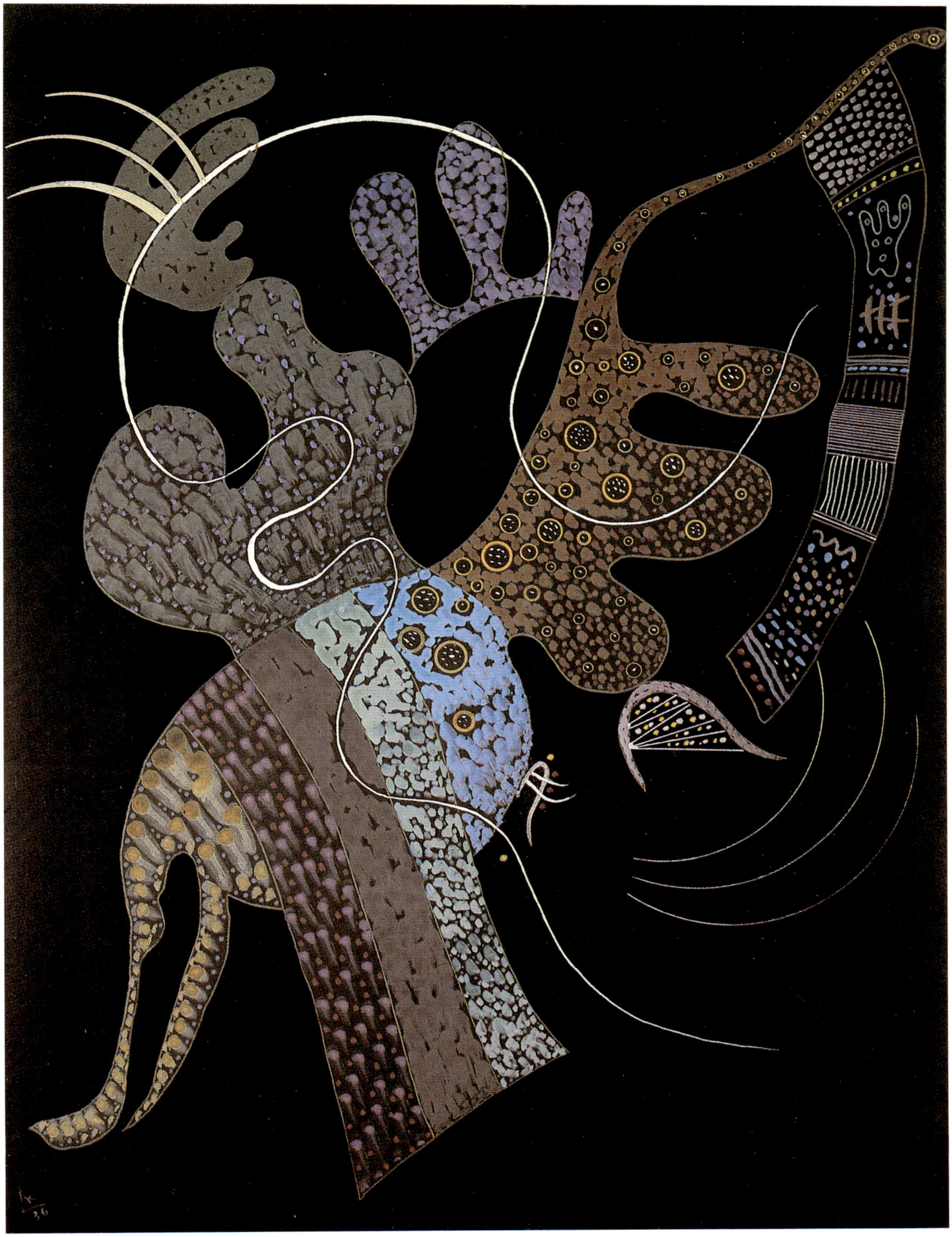

67

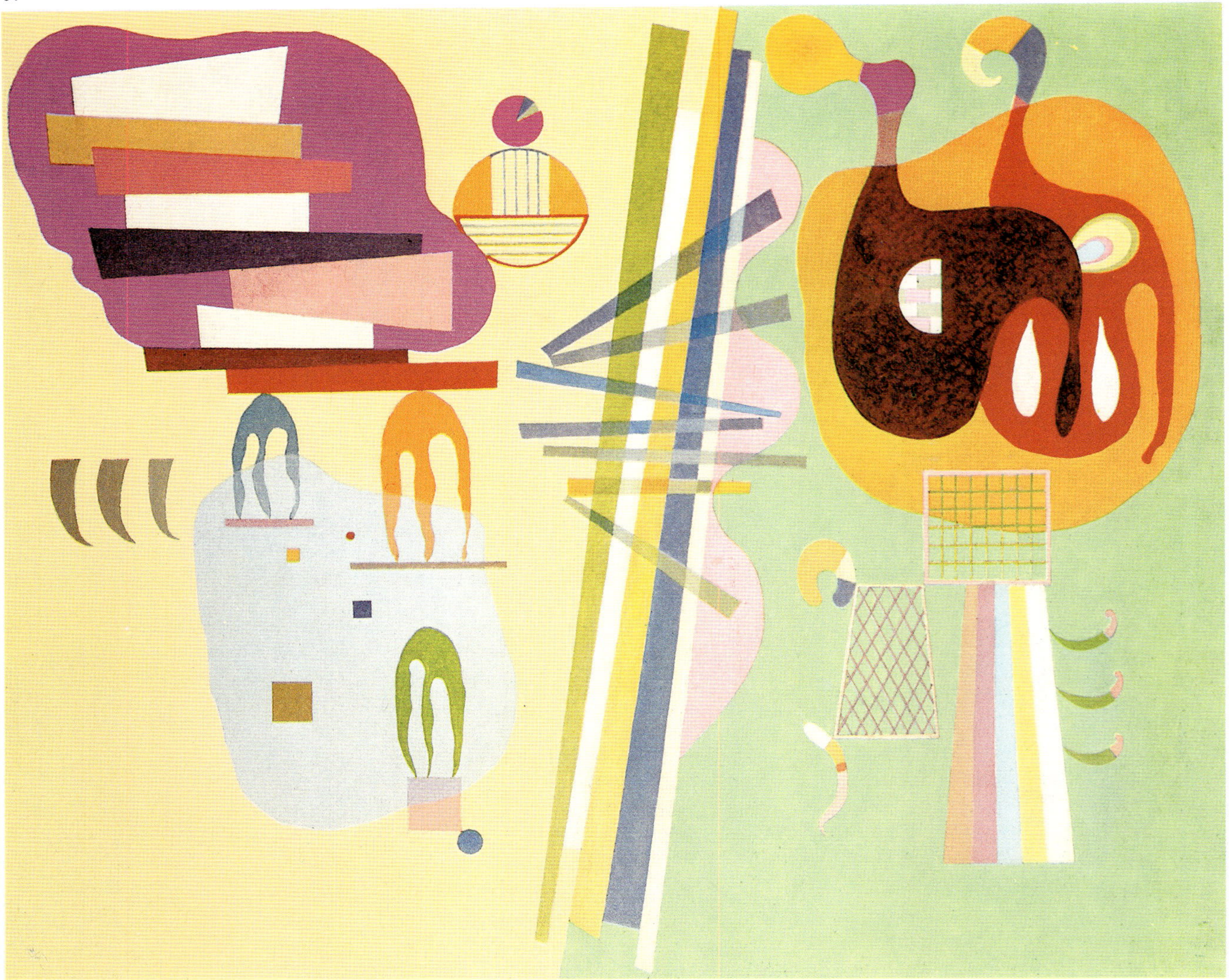

68

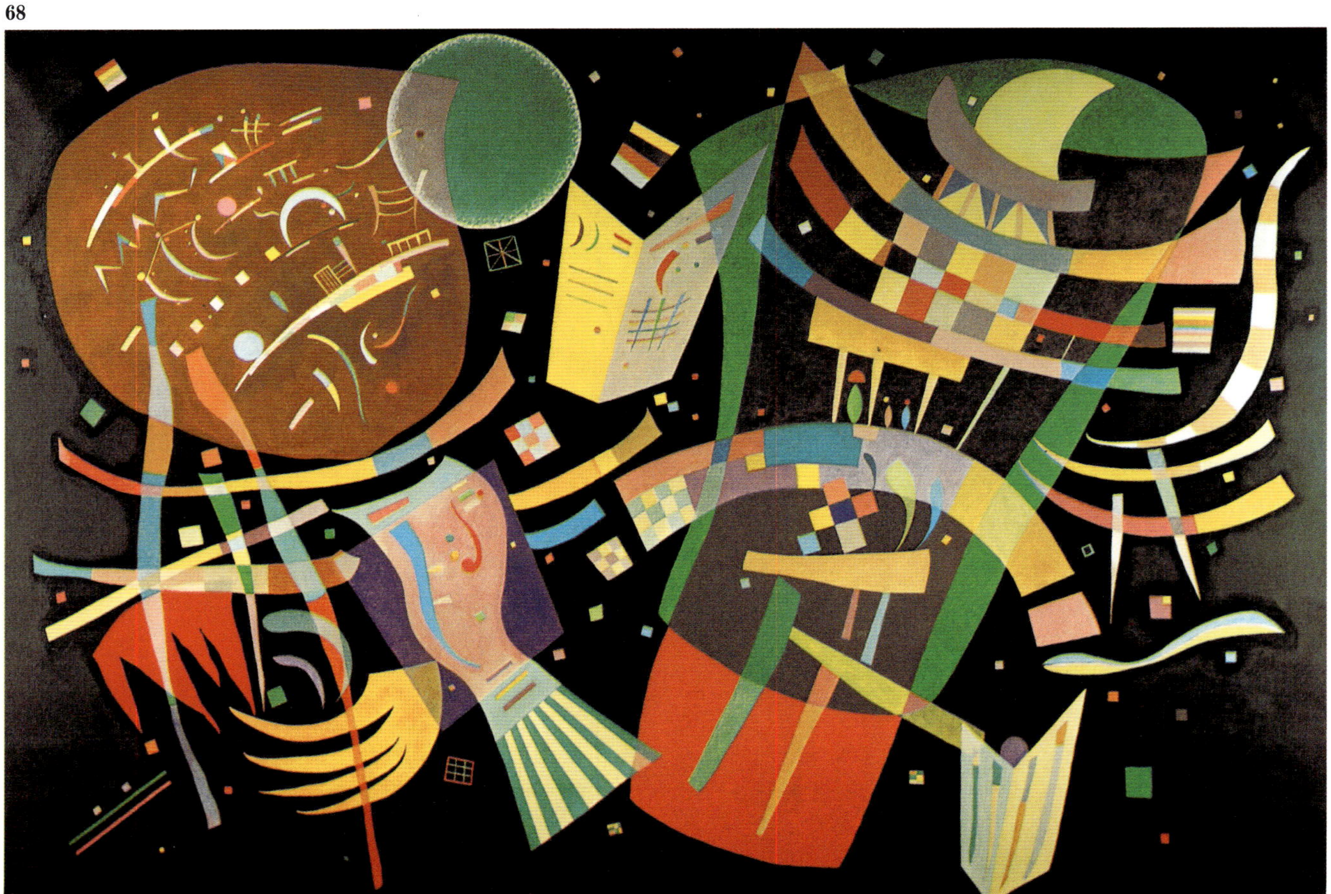

67 Unanimity, *1939. One of the most distinctive features of Kandinsky's last phase is the progressive lightening of his palette, which often became extremely bright, as well as his greater use of blended hues, lessening the reliance on primary colors that had extended through the Munich and Bauhaus years.*

68 Composition X, *1939. For Kandinsky, abstraction presupposed above all, the creation of an autonomous artistic universe, independent of nature, and yet no less real and concrete than the natural world. The colored shapes floating before a midnight background tell of just such an alternative and visionary universe.*

69 Sky Blue, *1940. The biomorphic forms seen here, looking like fantastic animals, may refer to the world of children's toys or to that of Slavic folk art, although Kandinsky was usually vexed when critics made such associations in talking about his work.*

69

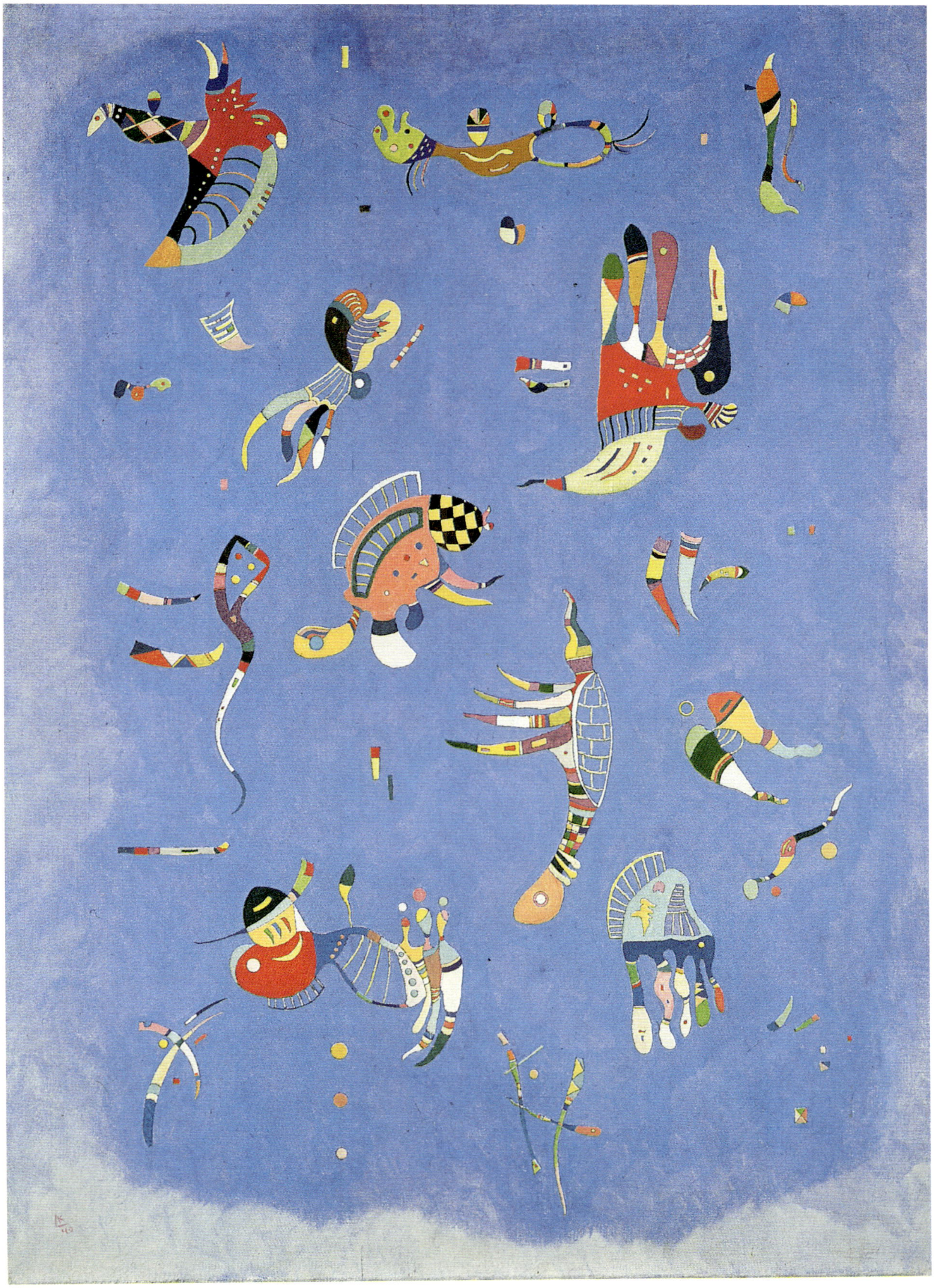

70

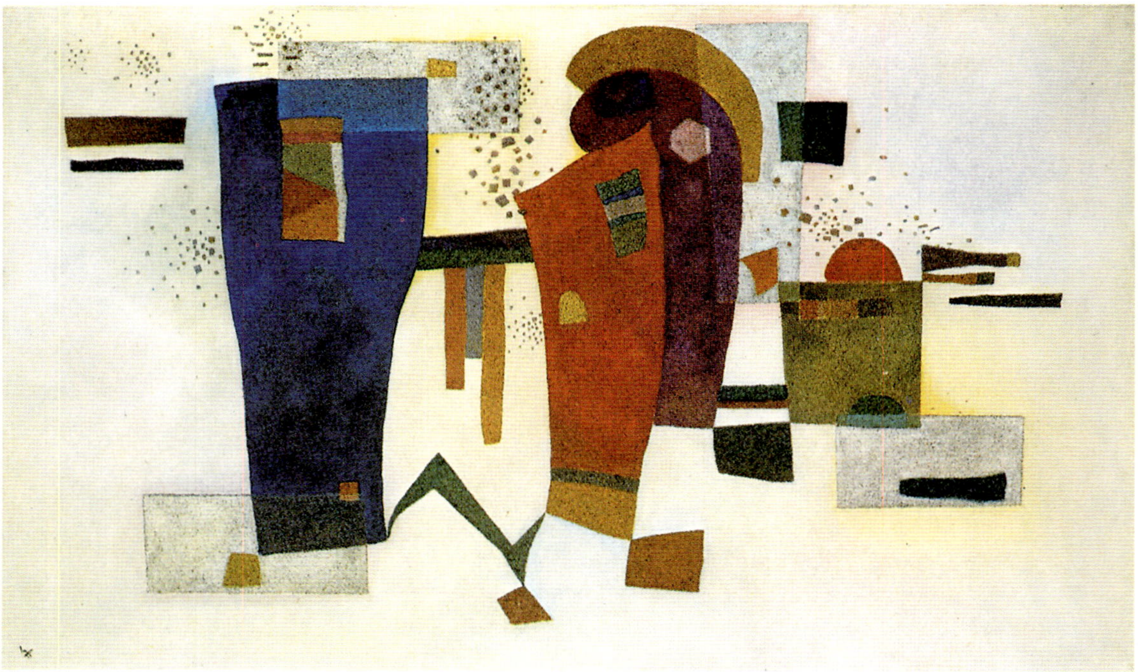

70 Accompanied Contrast, *1935. Generally not concerned with purely technical innovation, Kandinsky did nonetheless sometimes experiment with using sand to give texture to the paint.*

71 Delayed Actions, *1941. The freedom and fluidity of paintings such as this can make for quite an elaborate composition. A number of segments throughout the picture could easily have been developed into paintings in their own right. Indeed, many different parts of the canvas carry equal importance, without the focused cores of tension typical of the artist's earlier works.*

71

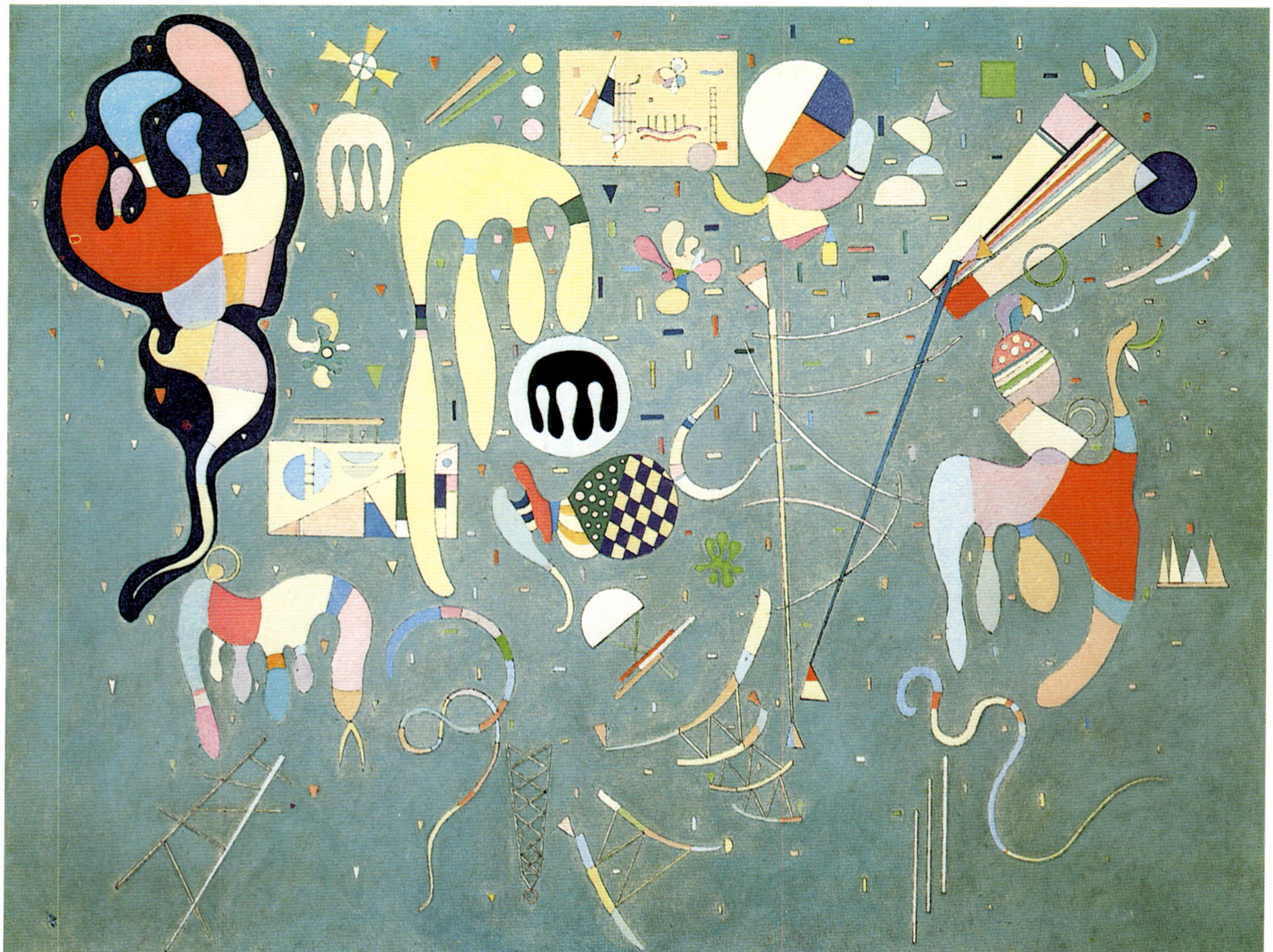

72, 73 Circle and Square, *1943;* The Small Red Circle, *1944. Kandinsky's last works, of which these are two examples, display certain devices from the geometric period, such as circles pierced by triangles, or the interaction between straight lines and curves generating the pictorial space. These are now presented in a different context, of course, but the artist remains loyal to the notion of an alternative painterly universe, only loosely connected to the material world.*

72

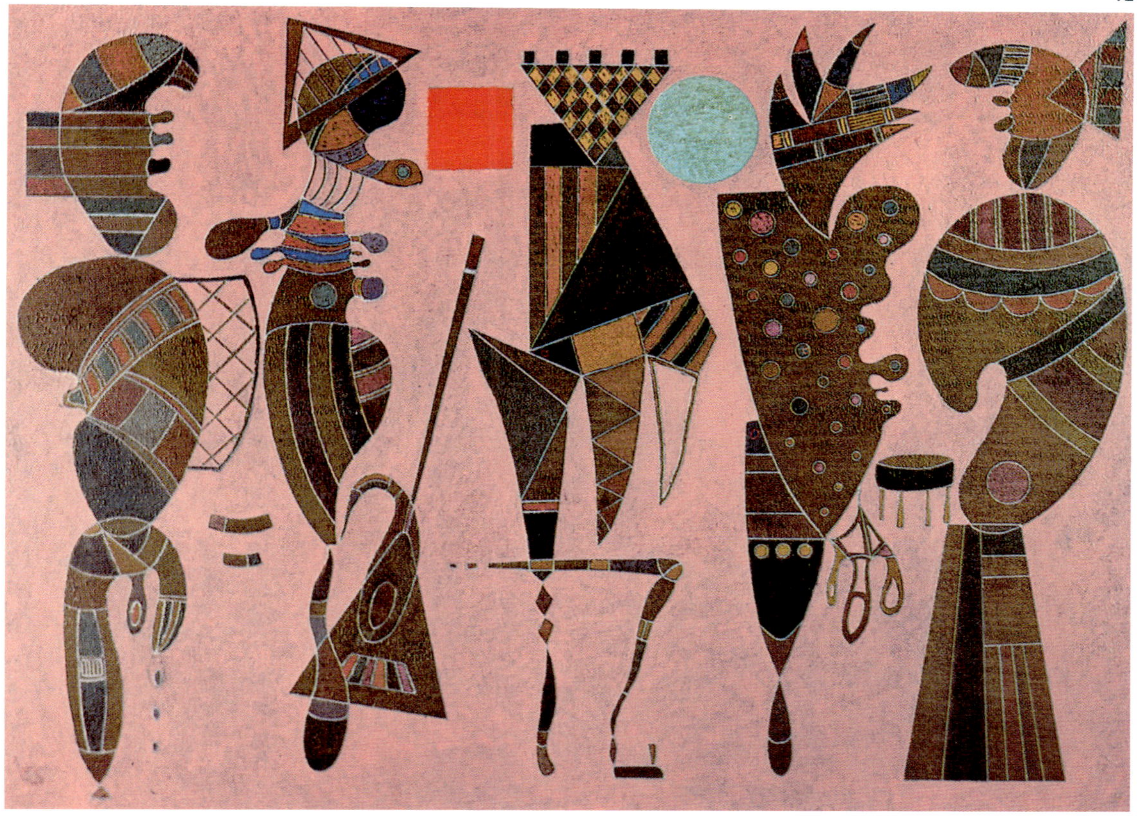

73

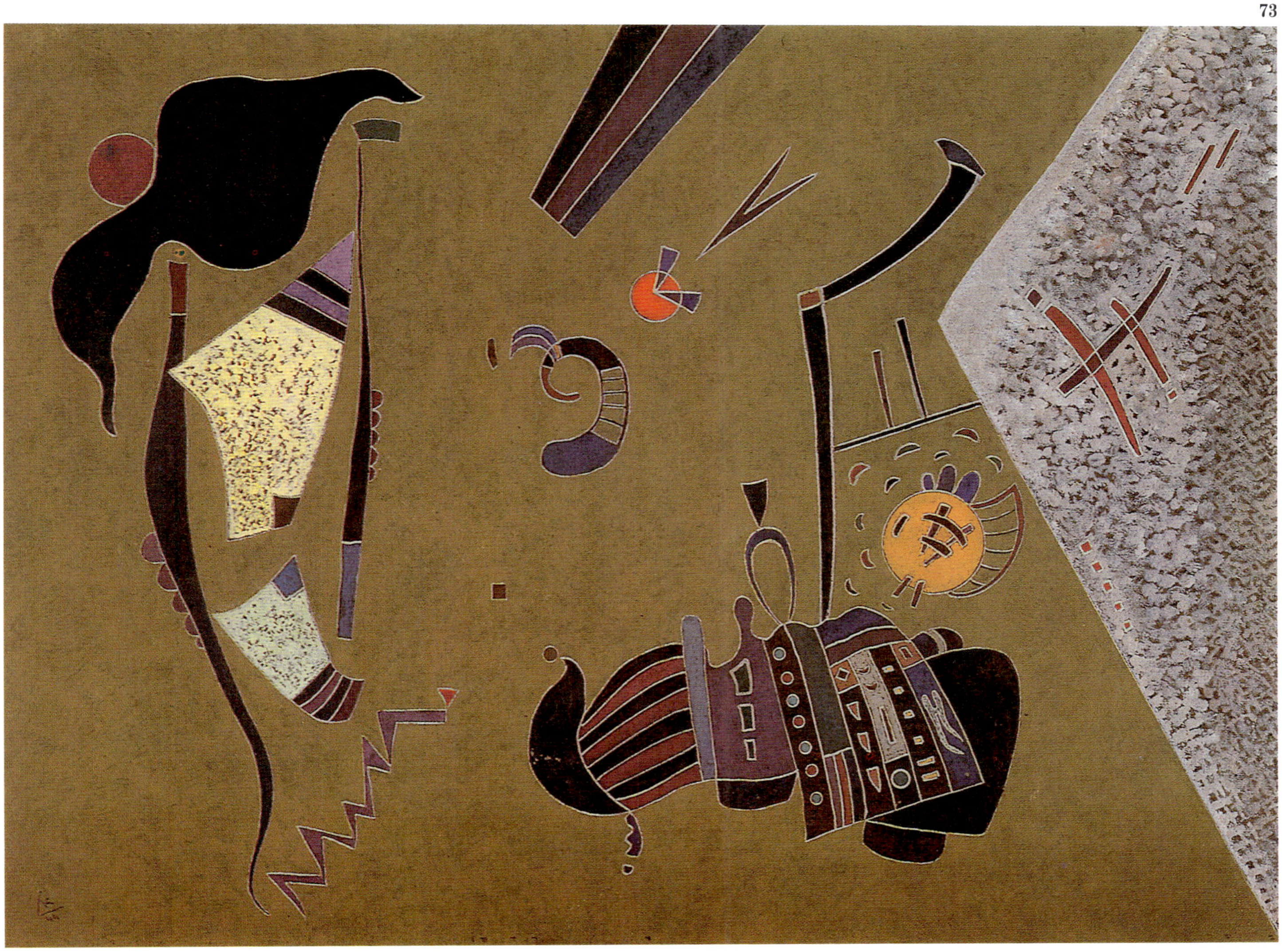

List of Plates

1 The Old City II, *1902. Oil on canvas, 20½ × 30⅞″ (52 × 78.2 cm). Musée National d'Art Moderne, Centre Georges Pompidou, Paris*

2 Kochel: Waterfall I, *1900. Oil on canvas over cardboard, 12¾ × 9¼″ (32.4 × 23.5 cm). Städtische Galerie, Munich*

3 Trees in Bloom at Lana, *1908. Oil on canvas over panel, 7 × 10⅛″ (17.8 × 25.9 cm). Private collection, New York*

4 Riegsee: The Town Church, *1908. Oil on cardboard, 13 × 17¾″ (33 × 45 cm). Von der Heydt-Museum, Wuppertal*

5 Munich: Schwabing with the Church of St. Ursula, *1908. Oil on cardboard, 27 × 19¼″ (68.8 × 49 cm). Städtische Galerie im Lenbachhaus, Munich*

6 Landscape with a Tower, *1908. Oil on cardboard, 29⅛ × 38¾″ (74 × 98.5 cm). Musée National d'Art Moderne, Centre Georges Pompidou, Paris*

7 Interior (My Dining Room), *1909. Oil on cardboard, 19⅝ × 25⅝″ (50 × 65 cm). Städtische Galerie im Lenbachhaus, Munich*

8 Oriental, *1909. Oil on cardboard, 27⅜ × 38″ (69.5 × 96.5 cm). Städtische Galerie im Lenbachhaus, Munich*

9 Mountain, *1909. Oil on canvas, 42⅞ × 42⅞″ (109 × 109 cm). Städtische Galerie im Lenbachhaus, Munich*

10 Obermarkt with Mountains, *1908. Oil on cardboard, 13 × 16⅛″ (33 × 41 cm). Private collection, Germany*

11 The Blue Rider, *1903. Oil on canvas, 21⅝ × 25½″ (55 × 65 cm). Private collection, Zurich*

12 *Sketch for* Achtyrka: Autumn, *1901. Oil on canvas over cardboard, 9⅜ × 12⅞″ (23.7 × 32.7 cm). Städtische Galerie im Lenbachhaus, Munich*

13 Riding Couple, *1906–7. Oil on canvas, 21⅝ × 19⅞″ (55 × 50.5 cm). Städtische Galerie im Lenbachhaus, Munich*

14 Portrait of Gabriele Münter, *1905. Oil on canvas, 17¾ × 17¾″ (45 × 45 cm). Städtische Galerie im Lenbachhaus, Munich*

15 Rapallo: Rough Sea, *1906. Oil on canvas over cardboard, 9 × 13″ (23 × 33 cm). Musée National d'Art Moderne, Centre Georges Pompidou, Paris*

16 The Farewell, *1903. Woodcut, 12⅜ × 12⅜″ (31.3 × 31.2 cm). Musée National d'Art Moderne, Centre Georges Pompidou, Paris*

17 Winter Landscape I, *1909. Oil on cardboard, 28⅛ × 38⅜″ (71.5 × 97.5 cm). The State Hermitage Museum, St. Petersburg*

18 Blue Mountain, *1908–9. Oil on canvas, 41¾ × 38″ (106 × 96.6 cm). Solomon R. Guggenheim Museum, New York*

19 Murnau: The Garden I, *1910. Oil on canvas, 26 × 32¾″ (66 × 82 cm). Städtische Galerie im Lenbachhaus, Munich*

20 Murnau: View with Railroad and Castle, *1909. Oil on cardboard, 14⅛ × 19¼″ (36 × 49 cm). Städtische Galerie im Lenbachhaus, Munich*

21 *Study for* Winter II, *1910–11. Oil on cardboard, 13 × 17½″ (33 × 44.7 cm). Städtische Galerie im Lenbachhaus, Munich*

22 *Sketch for* Composition II, *1910. Oil on canvas, 38⅜ × 51⅝″ (97.5 × 131.2 cm). Solomon R. Guggenheim Museum, New York*

23 Improvisation VI, *1909. Oil on canvas, 42⅛ × 39⅛″ (107 × 99.5 cm). Städtische Galerie im Lenbachhaus, Munich*

24 Improvisation VII, *1910. Oil on canvas, 51½ × 38⅛″ (131 × 97 cm). Tretyakov Gallery, Moscow*

25 Improvisation XVIII (with Tombstones), *1911. Oil on canvas, 55½ × 47¼″ (141 × 120 cm). Städtische Galerie im Lenbachhaus, Munich*

26 Improvisation XI, *1910. Oil on canvas, 38⅜ × 41⅞″ (97.5 × 106.5 cm). Russian Museum, St. Petersburg*

27 Passage by Boat, *1910. Oil on canvas, 38½ × 41⅜″ (98 × 105 cm). Tretyakov Gallery, Moscow*

28 Improvisation XIX, *1911. Oil on canvas, 47¼ × 55¾″ (120 × 141.5 cm). Städtische Galerie im Lenbachhaus, Munich*

29 All Saints' Day I, *1911. Oil on cardboard, 19⅝ × 25⅜″ (50 × 64.5 cm). Städtische Galerie im Lenbachhaus, Munich*

30 Autumn II, *1912. Oil on canvas, 23⅝ × 32¼″ (60 × 82 cm). The Phillips Collection, Washington, D.C*

31 Composition IV, *1911. Oil on canvas, 62⅞ × 8'2⅝″ (159.5 × 250.5 cm). Kunstsammlung Nordrhein-Westfalen, Düsseldorf*

32 Improvisation XIII, *1910. Oil on canvas, 47¼ × 55⅛″ (120 × 140 cm). Staatliche Kunsthalle, Karlsruhe*

33 Impression V (Park), *1911. Oil on canvas, 41¾ ×62″ (106 × 157.5 cm). Musée National d'Art Moderne, Centre Georges Pompidou, Paris*

34 St. George II, *1911. Oil on canvas, 42⅛ × 37¾″ (107 × 96 cm). Russian Museum, St. Petersburg*

35 Deluge I, *1912. Oil on canvas, 39⅜ × 41⅜″ (100 × 105 cm). Kaiser-Wilhelm Museum, Krefeld*

36 Improvisation XXVIII *(second version), 1912. Oil on canvas, 44½ × 62⅛″ (113 × 158 cm). Solomon R. Guggenheim Museum, New York*

37 Improvisation (Deluge), *1913. Oil on canvas, 37⅜ × 59″ (95 × 150 cm). Städtische Galerie im Lenbachhaus, Munich*

38 *Study for* Deluge II, *1912. Oil on canvas, 37⅜ × 42¼″ (95 × 107.5 cm). Collection Harold Diamont, New York*

39 Improvisation XXVI (Rowing), *1912. Oil on canvas, 38⅛ × 42¼″ (97 × 107.5 cm). Städtische Galerie im Lenbachhaus, Munich*

40 Painting with White Form, *1913. Oil on canvas, 47⅜ × 55″ (120.3 × 139.6 cm). Solomon R. Guggenheim Museum, New York*

41 Composition VI, *1913. Oil on canvas, 6'4¾″ × 10' (195 × 300 cm). The State Hermitage Museum, St. Petersburg*

42 Fantastic Improvisation, *1913. Oil on canvas, 51⅛ × 51⅛″ (130 × 130 cm). Städtische Galerie im Lenbachhaus, Munich*

43 Moscow II, *1916. Oil on canvas, 20½ × 14⅛″ (52 × 36 cm). Private collection*

44 Black Lines I, *1913. Oil on canvas, 51 × 51⅝″ (129.4 × 131.1 cm). Solomon R. Guggenheim Museum, New York*

45 Song of the Volga, *1906. Tempera on cardboard, 19¼ × 26″ (49 × 66 cm). Musée National d'Art Moderne, Centre Georges Pompidou, Paris*

46 Glass Painting with Sun, *1910. Reverse painting on glass with painted frame, 13½ × 16″ (34.5 × 40.5 cm). Städtische Galerie im Lenbachhaus, Munich*

47 All Saints' Day, *1911. Reverse painting on glass with painted frame, 12 × 15⅞″ (30.6 × 40.3 cm). Städtische Galerie im Lenbachhaus, Munich*

48 Woman in Moscow, *1912. Oil on canvas, 42⅞ × 42⅞″ (108.8 × 108.8 cm). Städtische Galerie im Lenbachhaus, Munich*

49 Last Judgment, *1912. Reverse painting on glass with painted frame, 13¼ × 17⅞″ (33.6 × 45.3 cm). Museé National d'Art Moderne, Centre Georges Pompidou, Paris*

50 Women in Crinoline, *1918. Reverse painting on glass, 9⅞ × 16″ (25.1 × 40.8 cm). Tretyakov Gallery, Moscow*

51 In the Gray, *1919. Oil on canvas, 50¾ × 69¼″ (129 × 176 cm). Musée National d 'Art Moderne, Centre Georges Pompidou, Paris*

52 White Line, *1920. Oil on canvas, 38½ × 31½″ (98 × 80 cm). Museum Ludwig, Cologne*

53 Red Oval, *1920. Oil on canvas, 28⅛ × 28″ (71.5 × 71.2 cm). Solomon R. Guggenheim Museum, New York*

54 Maquette of a Mural for the Unjuried Exhibition, *1922. Gouache on black paper, 13⅝ × 23⅝″ (34.7 × 60 cm). Museé National d'Art Moderne, Centre Georges Pompidou, Paris*

55 Black Pattern, *1922. Oil on canvas, 37¾ × 41¾″ (96 × 106 cm). Musée National d'Art Moderne, Centre Georges Pompidou, Paris*

56 Composition VIII, *1923. Oil on canvas, 55⅛ × 6'7⅛″ (140 × 201 cm). Solomon R. Guggenheim Museum, New York*

57 On White II, *1923. Oil on canvas, 41⅜ × 38⅝″ (105 × 98 cm). Musée National d'Art Moderne, Centre Georges Pompidou, Paris*

58 Still Tension, *1924. Oil on cardboard, 30⅞ × 21½″ (78.5 × 54.5 cm). Private collection, Paris*

59 Hard But Soft, *1927. Oil on canvas, 39⅜ × 19⅝″ (100 × 50 cm). Museum of Fine Arts, Boston*

60 Several Circles, *1926. Oil on canvas, 55⅛ × 55⅛″ (140 × 140 cm). Solomon R. Guggenheim Museum, New York*

61 Thirteen Rectangles, *1930. Oil on cardboard, 27⅜ × 23⅜″ (69.5 × 59.5 cm). Musée National d'Art Moderne, Centre Georges Pompidou, Paris*

62 Interrelations, *1934. Mixed mediums on canvas, 35 × 45⅝″ (89 × 116 cm). Collection Mr. and Mrs. David Lloyd Kreeger, Washington, D.C*

63 Graceful Ascent, *1934. Oil on canvas, 31½ × 31½″ (80 × 80 cm). Solomon R. Guggenheim Museum, New York*

64 Dominant Curve, *1936. Oil on canvas, 51⅛ × 6'4¾″ (130 × 195 cm). Solomon R. Guggenheim Museum, New York*

65 Accompanied Milieu, *1937. Oil on canvas, 44⅞ × 57½″ (114 × 146 cm). Whereabouts unknown. Formerly collection Adrien Maeght, Paris*

66 The White Line, *1936. Gouache and tempera on black paper, 19⅝ × 15¼″ (49.9 × 38.7 cm). Musée National d'Art Moderne, Centre Georges Pompidou, Paris*

67 Unanimity, *1939. Oil on canvas, 28¾ × 36¼″ (73 × 92 cm). Collection Jeffrey H. Loria, New York*

68 Composition X, *1939. Oil on canvas, 51⅛ × 6'4¾″ (130 × 195 cm). Kunstsammlung Nordrhein-Westfalen, Düsseldorf*

69 Sky Blue, *1940. Oil on canvas, 39⅜ × 28¾″ (100 × 73 cm). Musée National d'Art Moderne, Centre Georges Pompidou, Paris*

70 Accompanied Contrast, *1935. Oil with sand on canvas, 38⅛ × 63¾″ (97 × 162 cm). Solomon R. Guggenheim Museum, New York*

71 Delayed Actions, *1941. Mixed mediums on canvas, 35 × 45⅝″ (89 × 116 cm). Solomon R. Guggenheim Museum, New York*

72 Circle and Square, *1943. Tempera and oil on cardboard, 16½ × 22⅞″ (42 × 58 cm). Musée National d'Art Moderne, Centre Georges Pompidou, Paris*

73 The Small Red Circle, *1944. Gouache and oil on cardboard, 16½ × 22⅞″ (42 × 58 cm). Musée National d'Art Moderne, Centre Georges Pompidou, Paris*

Selected Bibliography

Avtonomova, Natalia, Vivian Endicott Barnett, et al. *New Perspectives on Kandinsky.* Malmö, Sweden: Malmö Konsthall, Sydsvenska Dagbladet, 1990.

Dabrowski, Magdalena. *Kandinsky: Compositions.* New York: The Museum of Modern Art, 1995.

Grohmann, Will. *Wassily Kandinsky: Life and Work.* New York: Harry N. Abrams, Inc., 1958.

Hahl-Koch, Jelena. *Kandinsky.* New York: Rizzoli, 1993.

Lindsay, Kenneth C., and Peter Vergo, eds. *Kandinsky: Complete Writings on Art.* Rev. ed., New York: Da Capo Press, 1994.

Roethel, Hans K., and Jean K. Benjamin. *Kandinsky: Catalogue Raisonne of the Oil Paintings. 2* vols. Ithaca, N.Y.: Cornell University Press, 1982, 1984.

Washton Long, Rose-Carol. *Kandinsky: The Development of an Abstract Style.* Oxford: Clarendon Press, 1980.

Weiss, Peg. *Kandinsky and "Old Russia": The Artist as Ethnographer and Shaman.* New Haven, Conn., and London: Yale University Press, 1995.